The Rockets' Red Glare:
The War of 1812 and Connecticut

New London County Historical Society
New London, Connecticut
2012

NEW LONDON
COUNTY HISTORICAL
SOCIETY

New London County Historical Society
11 Blinman Street
New London, CT 06320

Designed by Trish LaPointe, Old Mystic, CT
Printed by Signature Book Printing, www.sbpbooks.com

ISBN-13: 978-0-9853624-0-9
ISBN-10: 0-985-36240-5

Portions of Chapter 3, The Battle of Long Island Sound, appeared in James Tertius de Kay, *The Battle of Stonington: Torpedoes, Submarines, and Rockets in the War of 1812* (Annapolis: Naval Institute Press, 1990)

Meredith Mason Brown's sidebar, "The Reverend as Barometer: Connecticut's Conflicting Views of the War of 1812," appeared in slightly different form as "Why Do Ye Wrong One To Another: Stonington at the Start of the War of 1812," *Historical Footnotes: Bulletin of the Stonington Historical Society* 48, no. 3 (August 2010).

James Boylan's sidebar, "The Glorious Tenth: A Connecticut Town Remembers the War of 1812," originally appeared in *Historical Footnotes: Bulletin of the Stonington Historical Society* 36, no. 3 (August 1999).

Contents

Introduction

THE WAR OF 1812, HAS BEEN FORGOTTEN BY MANY AMERICANS, or seen as a footnote to the American pageant. Not so. It was, in truth, a pivotal event in the nation's development. Declared in June of 1812, its last climactic battle was fought in January of 1815, two weeks after peace negotiations ending the war were concluded. During the intervening years, citizens of the young United States had thrilled to stunning American victories against the strongest navy in the world, failed at numerous attempts to invade Canada, and suffered the ignominy of having their capitol city torched by British troops. As a result of the war, Americans also secured their northern and western borders and forever shattered Native American attempts to protect their trans-Appalachian homelands. Back east, the whaling, fishing, and merchant fleets were devastated, while the seeds of America's industrial might took root. Meanwhile internal dissent and rumors of secession challenged the political viability of the fledgling republic. The year 1812 saw the start of a war that should never be forgotten.

Some of the dynamics of 1812 will feel familiar to Americans of the early twenty-first century. The world two hundred years ago was in flux. Competing beliefs and systems of governance were struggling for dominance, and Americans were divided in their response to that struggle. Some Americans, particularly those on the western frontier and along the east coast, were all too familiar with the pain and sorrow that comes with war. At the turn of the nineteenth century, the American War for Independence was a very recent memory, and many communities, including Connecticut's New Haven, Norwalk, Danbury, New London, and Groton had suffered for their newly won freedom. Meanwhile, the War for Independence had sparked a period that is still known as the Age of Revolution in European history. Conflict raged on the other side of the Atlantic two hundred years ago; uncertainty was the hallmark of the era. With the advent of war in 1812, the United States found itself overmatched at sea, and Congress determined to embrace asymmetrical warfare. An 1813 Act of Congress promised ample remuneration to "any person or persons" using "any . . . destructive machines whatever" to destroy vessels of the Royal Navy. This attempt was, by and large, carried out on the shores of Connecticut, and the residents of the state's eastern communities paid the price for the use of terror. There, with the sea at their doorstep, nutmeggers were confronted with the causes of the war and the consequences of it as well. Depredations and restrictions against the shipping of New London County serve to highlight the nation's slide toward war, just as British attacks on Essex, Mystic, Stonington, and numerous ports further up Long Island Sound, exemplify the belligerents' strengths and weaknesses.

This book was prepared as a companion to the exhibit, *The Rockets' Red Glare: Connecticut and the War of 1812—A Bicentennial Exhibit*, held at the Lyman Allyn Art Museum in New London, Connecticut, during the summer and fall of 2012. The book, and the exhibit, examine the ways the War of 1812 relate to the state of Connecticut and its coastal region, in part through its material culture—the physical remains of that era held in some of the region's collections—as well as through an analysis of the experiences and words of its defenders. This will be done within the context of the much larger national experience.

This volume is divisible into six distinct, but interconnected elements. Chapters 1, 2, and 5, written by Glenn S. Gordinier, seek to put Connecticut into the larger context of the era of the War of 1812. The opening chapter examines the international environment in which the United States operated, and the policies and debates that eventually led the nation to declare war. Chapter 2 offers an overview of the various campaigns and cruises that surrounded Connecticut and its wartime affairs. Gordinier's concluding chapter tracks the end of the war and considers its impacts on Connecticut, and the legacy it left to ensuing generations of Americans.

Chapter 3, by James Tertius de Kay, is drawn in large part from his comprehensive book, *The Battle of Stonington*, published by the Naval Institute Press in 1990. De Kay's work about warfare on Long Island Sound illustrates how conflict on the Sound eventually led to its most spectacular, if not strategically important event, the bombardment of the village of Stonington in August 1814. Chapter 4 is edited by Dr. Nancy Steenburg, whose current research regards nineteenth-century historian and author Frances Manwaring Caulkins. An amateur historian who was thorough in her scholarship, Caulkins published very reliable and informative histories of both Norwich and New London, Connecticut. Steenburg has found Caulkins's 1828 manuscript account of her interviews with those who actually fought to defend Stonington 14 years earlier. Caulkins's words and Steenburg's annotations elucidate what happened in Stonington during the British attack.

The fifth element of this volume is the creation of Fred Calabretta, curator of collections at Mystic Seaport. His work is seen in two sidebar essays and the captions for the numerous illustrations he organized for this book, most of which are of objects selected for display in *The Rockets' Red Glare* exhibit.

The text is augmented with extensive sidebar essays written by other experts on Connecticut's experience in the War of 1812. These authors, Stonington's James Boylan, and Meredith Mason Brown, the Connecticut River Museum's Jerry Roberts, and Central Connecticut States University's Dr. Matthew Warshauer, have all offered their expertise to help round out this Connecticut story and give it a personal face. Their sidebars will provide insights about enemy incursions, homeland defenders, privateers, political dissent and patriotic memory. Several other sidebars, including pieces on Connecticut privateers and the experience of Mrs. James Stewart, wife of the British consul, were penned by Mystic's Andrew W. German, whose talents as a researcher, contributor, and this volume's editor have been vital to the completion of this project.

The Rockets' Red Glare exhibit and book are the products of a collaboration between a number of local organizations and individuals. Thanks go to the Stonington Historical Society, Mystic Seaport, the New London Maritime Society and Custom House Museum, the New London County Historical Society, and the Lyman Allyn Art Museum for their efforts. We also would like to acknowledge the assistance of a variety of people who contributed directly or indirectly to the completion of this project. Thanks go out to the committee members who have worked so diligently to bring this collaborative effort to fruition: Meredith Mason Brown, former president of the Stonington Historical Society; Mystic Seaport's Fred Calabretta; Director Susan Tamulevich of the New London Maritime Society; and at the Lyman Art Allyn Museum, Director Nancy Stula and Registrar and Assistant Curator Carolyn Grosch. We are also pleased to acknowledge the expertise of those who helped bring the exhibit and book to their successful conclusion: exhibit script writer Fred Calabretta; exhibit designer Jeff Crewe; textile conservator Susan Jerome; and Tricia Royston, librarian for the New London County Historical Society. Our appreciation also goes out to Tom Althuis of the

Groton Bank Historical Association, Munson Institute graduate Joseph Greene, and research assistants Vera Cecelski and Gregory Conyers of the Williams College/Mystic Seaport Program in Maritime Studies for their detective work. The talents of book designer Trish LaPointe also deserve to be acknowledged. Particular thanks go out to Edward Baker, Executive Director of the New London County Historical Society, who put this collaborative voyage in motion and has stood at the helm for the disparate crew throughout.

This volume's research, writing and design and its companion exhibit were made possible by grants from the Connecticut Humanities Council. Our gratitude also goes out to the Coby Foundation of New York for their support for the exhibition of textiles. Special thanks are due Robert and Cynthia Martin for their generous support of this volume.

Glenn S. Gordinier
Stonington, CT

CHAPTER ONE

Profits, Tensions, and Neutral Trade

CONNECTICUT AND THE REST OF THE NEW United States struggled to find a free and unified place in the world after the Treaty of Paris ended the American Revolution in 1783. The Constitutional Convention of 1787 hammered out a system for political unity that incorporated the interests of all the states, large and small, North and South. Through the debates over this new government and its establishment under President George Washington in 1789, two positions or parties took shape: the Federalists who followed Alexander Hamilton in the desire for an economy based on manufacturing and foreign trade; and the Republicans, who followed Thomas Jefferson in the belief in an agrarian economy with limited involvement in the wider world.

The nation's economy, however, could not be legislated into good health. Throughout the United States, destruction of war, soaring inflation, and widespread debt left the populace struggling. In Connecticut, the effects of British raids on Danbury, Norwalk, New Haven, and New London could still be seen. In Groton, the impact of the September 1781 assault on Fort Griswold would be felt for decades. The slaughter of nearly 80 defenders in the "Massacre at Fort Griswold" left many local families without fathers, brothers, and sons—breadwinners—who would be missed for a lifetime and beyond.[1]

Through the 1780s and 1790s, Connecticut merchants struggled to reestablish trade routes. On the one hand Connecticut's exchange of goods and produce between coastal ports—especially New York—returned quickly. But on the high seas British protectionist trade policies excluded American vessels from their former markets in the British West Indies. The ships, brigs, schooners, and sloops that carried Connecticut's foreign trade sought new opportunities in the French West Indies, Spain, Portugal, Amsterdam, Ireland, and Liverpool.[2] Larger ports, including Boston, New York, and Philadelphia, sent their vessels to even more distant trading ports: Calcutta, India; Batavia in the Dutch East Indies; St. Petersburg and Archangel, Russia; and Canton, China.

Built at Haddam, Connecticut, in 1805, the ship *Abula* sailed out of New York as a neutral trader. Marine artist Nicolas Cammillieri painted this view of her arriving at Marseilles, France, in May 1806, with her typical mix of white and black sailors busy taking in sail.

(© Mystic Seaport Collection, Mystic, CT, #1975.448)

Ship Abula. Cap.ⁿ John Dillingham entering the Port of Marseilles May 10. 1806

This spirit of maritime enterprise is personified by John Ledyard of Groton. While serving as a marine in the Pacific under the great British explorer, Captain James Cook, Ledyard had seen the value of sea otter pelts in the China market. Back home, he failed to convince local merchants to invest in an expedition to the Pacific Northwest and then on to Canton to make their fortunes, but he influenced the New York and Philadelphia entrepreneurs who underwrote America's first China voyage. In time, Boston merchants realized Ledyard's vision on the Northwest Coast, but by then Ledyard was off across Siberia and into Africa in search of adventure and profit.[3]

In February of 1793, the new French Republic declared war against France's longtime rival Great Britain. The conflict would continue almost unabated for the next 22 years. That widespread and long-lived war presented America with opportunities, challenges, and eventually bloodshed.

For the first 19 years, America remained neutral. Although most of the nation's leadership might favor one belligerent over the other—Federalists leaning toward Britain, and Republicans toward France—the foreign policy of the country was to avoid taking sides. This allowed American merchant vessels to carry cargoes to or from either belligerent and its colonies. For the most part, this meant carrying sugar or molasses to Europe from the Caribbean. This trade was vital to both of the warring nations to feed their people and fund their war efforts.

Flouting their neutrality in the conflict, American ships almost immediately began carrying goods for the combatants, who soon came to rely on them as links to their distant colonies. Sometimes American farmers benefitted from neutral trade as well. In the 1798 "Glorious First of June" battle, the Royal Navy defeated a French fleet on the high seas. However, a convoy of American vessels loaded with grain and flour from New York and Pennsylvania slipped past the British warships and arrived

Launched at Boston in 1797, the USS *Constitution* was one of the six new frigates that represented the United States on the high seas through the war of 1812. The wartime service and successes of ships such as the USS *Constitution* fueled storied reputations, influencing the future development of the US Navy and enhancing its status as an enduring symbol and source of national pride. This model was built by H.W. Chaloner about 1920. Mr. Chaloner was by trade a cabinetmaker and maintained a shop in Boston. His model not only *represents* an iconic American fighting ship, its base is fabricated from wood salvaged from the actual ship.

(© Mystic Seaport Collection, Mystic, CT, #1945.834)

in France, preventing bread riots in Paris and preserving the French government.[4]

The war expanded Connecticut's trade to the sugar islands of the Caribbean. Both the British and the French islands needed to import the products of Southern New England's fields, forests, and sea: fish, timber, and farm products like butter, cheese, beef, pork, tallow candles, onions, and Indian corn. Most importantly, however, the vessels that cleared New London carried horses, oxen, and mules. Just as New England salt cod was needed to feed the enslaved work force of the Caribbean, a steady stream of live animals was needed to move heavy loads and to fertilize the sugar fields with manure. By 1807, $250,000 worth of livestock went from eastern Connecticut to the islands annually. The vessels and the men who ran them were appropriately known as "horse jockeys."[5] With a deck measuring perhaps 50 feet long by 20 feet wide, these seagoing barnyards carried horses, cattle, and oxen in crude stalls on deck. Too often during their two-week passages to the islands, storms at sea cost investors some or all of their livestock as they lost their footing on a rolling deck, fell, and were unable to right themselves, sometimes drowning on deck.[6] Yet, this harsh and unlikely trade provided much of the capital to invest in the valuable sugar cargoes that helped bring prosperity to Connecticut during the age of neutral trade.

Challenges to American neutral traders on the high seas pushed the nation to both diplomatic and military expansion. British seizures of American vessels declined with the passage of the Jay Treaty, ratified in 1796 at the behest of the Federalists. France saw this accommodation with Great Britain as a betrayal and began to seize American merchant vessels and seamen. These Franco-American tensions resulted in a two-year, undeclared "Quasi War." As a result, the nation's high-seas navy was rushed into being with the launch of the frigates *Constitution, United States,* and *Constellation* in 1797. This naval

Connecticut's Arms-Makers

written by Andrew W. German

OTHER THAN BUILDING a few gunboats, Connecticut shipyards did not participate in the construction of the US Navy, but Connecticut manufacturers became leaders in supplying the new nation's military.

The ironworks at Salisbury, in the northwest corner of the state, had begun producing munitions during the American Revolution. Cannons cast there were used widely during the war, and decades later they were scattered among defenses around the nation for federal and state use. In southeastern Connecticut, Stonington housed two 18-pounders cast at Salisbury in 1781. The ironworks no longer produced cannons, but it continued to cast iron cannonballs.

With the likelihood of war with France increasing, in 1798 Congress authorized funds to purchase arms from private manufacturers. Several Connecticut men obtained contracts and became the leading producers of American military weapons.

After spending time in Georgia, where he invented the cotton gin, Yale graduate Eli Whitney settled in New Haven. Losing money to legal wrangling about his cotton gin, Whitney hoped to recoup his fortune by obtaining a government contract to manufacture more than 10,000 muskets for delivery in 1800. He received a large advance in 1798 and built an armory in New Haven, but manufacturing problems—Whitney had no experience in gunsmithing—delayed delivery until 1809. With much smaller contracts, Abijah Peck of Hartford and Amos Stillman of Farmington delivered their government muskets on time.

Simeon North of Berlin, Connecticut, had manufactured little but farm implements before he obtained a contract in 1799 to produce 500 horse pistols for the army. He modeled his efficient brass and iron flintlock on a French model. A second contract for 1,500 horse pistols was followed in 1808 with a contract for 2,000 boarding pistols for the navy.

Although Eli Whitney has long been credited as the first to create interchangeable parts while manufacturing his muskets, it was many years before he successfully mastered the method he espoused. More than Whitney, it was Simeon North who refined and applied efficient methods of production that led to interchangeability. In 1813 he would accept a contract for 20,000 pistols that called for almost perfect interchangeability of parts. To produce these arms on a truly industrial scale, he would move his factory to Middletown.[1]

Already in Middletown was Nathan Starr, a sythe-maker who had served as an armorer during the Revolutionary War. Starr received a contract for 2,000 cavalry sabers, scabbards, and belts in 1798, which made him the nation's first sword manufacturer since the Revolution. He also produced several thousand naval cutlasses in 1799 and 1808, between additional federal and state contracts for sabers. He and his son remained the leading manufacturers of American swords until 1830.[2]

When America went to war, the products of Connecticut arms-makers would be heavily represented on land and on sea. And the methods they developed to produce these weapons would contribute to the growth of industrialization in America.

war was largely fought in West Indian waters and proved the new US Navy to be surprisingly capable.

When the new president, Thomas Jefferson, refused to continue paying tribute to the Barbary State of Tripoli in North Africa, Tripoli declared war on the US in 1801. The US Navy sailed to the Mediterranean and gained much more fighting experience during the four-year war. In a particularly daring exploit, a small force led by the dashing Lieutenant Stephen Decatur destroyed the captured frigate *Philadelphia*. British Admiral Lord Horatio Nelson called this "the most bold and daring act of the age," and Decatur became the toast of the nation.

The maritime merchants of New England were, almost to a man, Federalists. In eastern Connecticut their local leader was General Jedidiah Huntington of the wealthy and influential Norwich family. Huntington and his associates represented the "Standing Order": ardent Congregationalists, powerful in the Connecticut Assembly, Federalist in politics.[7] A personal friend and wartime associate of George Washington, Huntington had been appointed collector of customs for the New London customs district in 1789. This was a high honor, as Washington only selected men he knew would be trusted by their communities when a nation born of tax protest turned to tax its own. In an age when customs duties financed almost all government expenses, Huntington served faithfully and well until 1815.

Accounts kept by Jedidiah Huntington and his fellow customs collectors document the prosperity brought through neutral trade. The value of America's foreign trade increased from $57,000,000 in 1793 to $247,000,000 in 1807. That explosion in the volume of imports and exports called for more American vessels to carry those neutral cargoes, and the American fleet expanded from 520,000 tons in 1793 to 1,270,000 tons in 1807.[8] All of those vessels, and all of those arrivals and departures, meant a corresponding growth in work for sailors, shipbuilders, sailmakers, block-makers, coopers, business agents, and entrepreneurs. And their prosperity added wealth to their communities. From Stonington to Norwalk, and up the Connecticut River as far as Windsor, Connecticut ports large and small were a part of this boom.[9] Many of America's fine Federal-style homes were built on the foundation of neutral trade.

This prosperity did not come without a cost, however. A voyage to the French West Indies meant that Royal Navy cruisers could seize the American vessel if it was found to be carrying French goods, unless the American captain could prove that he was not supporting the wartime French economy, but was involved in innocent neutral trade. American vessels carrying British goods might be seized by French cruisers when visiting European continental ports.

Taking advantage of a 1798 British ruling, American shipowners devised a strategy to help them avoid capture. By international understanding, if a vessel was carrying cargo to or from a neutral port, the ship and cargo would be considered neutral as well, no matter the point of origin or the ultimate destination. By adding an American port of call between the West Indies and Europe, shipowners could claim the goods as neutral. This strategy was called the "broken voyage." New London-area shipowners practiced their own version of the broken voyage, sending their brigs and schooners to the French island of Martinique, then back to New London, both of which were neutral passages. Then the French sugar and molasses were shipped from New London to New York and carried on to France.[10] In all cases the passages were neutral. Had they gone directly from Martinique to France, they risked seizure by British cruisers.

In the summer of 1805, a British Admiralty Court decided in the case of the American ship *Essex* that the broken voyage would no longer be honored. She had been seized by the Royal Navy while carrying goods of a French ally after a stop in the US, and the *Essex* Decision, as it came to be known, changed the face of trade in the Atlantic World. By year's end the Royal Navy dominated the seaways of the Atlantic following Admiral Lord Nelson's overwhelming victory at Trafalgar, while Napoleon's armies would secure his control of Europe with his victory at Austerlitz. The space between these superpowers narrowed with the *Essex* Decision, and America's merchant fleet would suffer as a result.

In its campaign to end American carriage of French sugar and molasses, the British Royal Navy patrolled near the French Caribbean islands and along the American coast itself. Royal Navy cruisers took position just off New York or Chesapeake Bay and, at their leisure, stopped and inspected any vessel they chose, whether for suspicious behavior or, it seemed, for sport. Hundreds of American vessels were forced to heave to, at times in territorial waters, to have their cargoes and their crews inspected.

The inspection of crewmembers was a particularly galling invasion of American sovereignty. Great Britain asserted that Britons could never give up their citizenship so they were always liable for impressment into the Royal Navy, even if they had become naturalized Americans. Without identifying papers, American-born mariners might be impressed into the service of the king as well. For its part, the Royal Navy claimed that its deserters populated the American merchant marine by the thousands. Conservative estimates suggest that perhaps 10,000 Americans were impressed between 1793 and 1812.[11] American diplomats attempted to negotiate an end to impressment, but neither side would accommodate to the other's position.

When the US frigate *Chesapeake* departed Norfolk on a routine cruise in June of 1807, she was stopped by HMS *Leopard*. British deserters were believed to have joined the American crew, so a British lieutenant boarded the *Chesapeake* and demanded that the crew be mustered for inspection. Commodore James Barron naturally refused such an outrageous request. The *Leopard* then fired several broadsides into the unprepared American frigate. With dead and wounded covering his decks, Barron was forced to lower his flag. Four men—only one of whom proved to be an English deserter—were removed to the *Leopard*.

When the damaged and humiliated *Chesapeake* returned to Norfolk, the populace was enraged. President Jefferson sought compensation, not war as some demanded. However, Jefferson did demand that all Royal Navy vessels leave the American coast. The British refused, and America's inability to force them from its waters only emphasized Yankee impotence in the face of British naval might.[12]

Yet, neutral trade remained so profitable that the American merchant marine flourished despite losing approximately 200 vessels a year. The New London Customs District saw its fleet grow by 37 percent between 1801 and 1807, while the import duties collected for the same period nearly quadrupled.[13]

By November 1807, both Britain and France were trying desperately to strangle the economy of the other by further restricting neutral trade. Unable to influence France, or especially Great Britain, to respect American neutral rights, President Jefferson, with the support of the Republicans in Congress, took a radical step. On December 22, 1807, he signed into law "An act laying an embargo on all ships and vessels in the ports and harbors of the United States." While some called for war, he chose the peaceful strategy of embargo, hoping that the absence of the cargoes previously delivered by American neutral traders would be enough of an economic hardship to persuade British or French policymakers to lift the restrictions on American traders.

Under the embargo, the federal government and the military worked to impound the whole of the nation's foreign trading fleet. At the forefront of this effort were the customs collectors assigned to the nation's seventy-odd customs districts. Connecticut had four customs districts: New London,

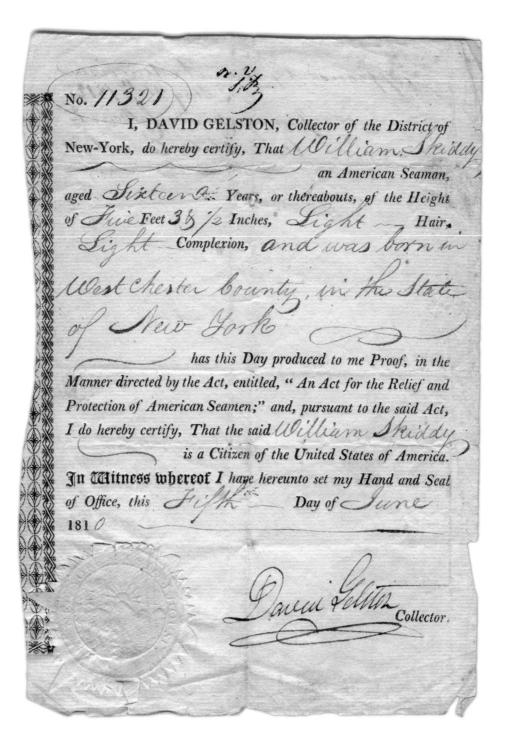

No. 11321

I, DAVID GELSTON, Collector of the District of New-York, do hereby certify, That *William Skiddy* an American Seaman, aged *Sixteen* Years, or thereabouts, of the Height of *Five* Feet *3½* Inches, *Light* Hair, *Light* Complexion, *and was born in West Chester County, in the State of New York* has this Day produced to me Proof, in the Manner directed by the Act, entitled, "An Act for the Relief and Protection of American Seamen;" and, pursuant to the said Act, I do hereby certify, That the said *William Skiddy* is a Citizen of the United States of America. In Witness whereof I have hereunto set my Hand and Seal of Office, this *Fifth* Day of *June* 1810

David Gelston
Collector.

American seaman William T. Skiddy (1795-1870) spent part of his boyhood in Stamford, Connecticut, the home of his ship-captain stepfather John R. Skiddy. William went to sea in 1805 at the age of ten and remained in the merchant service until 1812. In 1796, Congress had passed An Act for the Protection and Relief of American Seamen, which called for the issue of protection certificates to verify the identity and nationality of American sailors to prevent their impressment by the Royal Navy. New York Customs Collector David Gelston issued Skiddy's protection certificate in 1810, when impressment was a partic-ularly contentious issue.

(© Mystic Seaport, William T. Skiddy Collection (Coll. 304), Mystic, CT)

Middletown, New Haven, and Fairfield. To assist in the effort, New London Collector Huntington had the revenue cutter *Argus.* New Haven Collector Abraham Bishop relied on the cutter *Eagle.*

Although much of America's merchant marine was left idle and rotting in suddenly quiet ports, some merchants worked around the embargo. Many vessels from Massachusetts smuggled goods to Canadian markets, while Southern shipping slipped across the border to Spanish Florida. Eastern Connecticut merchants attempted other strategies, including moving vessels from foreign trade to the domestic coasting trade and, most importantly, taking advantage of a loophole in the Embargo Act that permitted them to send vessels to the West Indies under licenses from Customs Collector Jedidiah Huntington, a political opponent of Jefferson's Republican Democrats.[14]

The embargo lasted 14 months. Although it had little effect on British and French policymakers, it nearly brought down the American economy. Medium-size and smaller ports, including most of those in Connecticut, never rebounded as foreign trading ports.

Having failed to coerce the warring nations, in 1809 Congress passed a non-intercourse act by which American ships would return to sea to trade with all nations except Britain and France. When this failed to influence them, in 1810 Congress passed Macon's Bill No. 2, which promised that America would trade with everyone, including the French and British, until one or the other stopped seizing American ships, at which point the US would trade exclusively with that nation. This strategy resulted in Napoleon's apparent promise to give ground. Yet, the French continued to seize American vessels, even as America's proposed alignment with France heightened tensions with Great Britain.

Adding to America's tendency to focus on Britain as its enemy is what has recently been identified as "conspiratorial Anglophobia." This mindset appealed to people from the West, the North, the South, and the coast, who otherwise had little in common. Fear of a vast British conspiracy to constrain and then dominate the young republic's manufacturing, shipping, banking, and western expansion played into the hands of policymaking Anglophobes, who beat a steady tattoo upon the public imagination.[15]

CHAPTER TWO

War Comes to the Nation

BY THE EARLY MONTHS OF 1812, the frustrated Republic had identified its "enemy" as Great Britain, with its powerful navy. But the British Parliament was actually moving toward negotiation with the United States, as trade restrictions had begun to impact British industry. War might have been avoided, but the prime minister was assassinated in May 1812, and by the time Parliament addressed the issue again, it was too late.

When Congress took its war vote in June of 1812, it did so largely along party lines. The Federalists, mostly from northern and eastern states, voted to a man against the declaration of war. Over 80 percent of the Republicans, largely from Pennsylvania, the South, and the West, voted for war. The list of grievances against Great Britain made it clear that maritime concerns led to the vote. Topping the list were impressment of American seamen and British restrictions on American shipping. Grievances included British blockades and violation of American sovereignty in coastal waters, both of which diminished the nation's maritime freedoms and its national pride. Congress also expressed concern about the British inciting Native-American violence against settlers in the West. However, Indian violence was essentially independent of British interests, and in direct response to unrelenting American incursions into native lands. Although early campaigns against Canadian territory suggest that a Canadian land grab was a central aim of the war, this was not the case. American invasions of Canadian territory were war strategies, not war goals.[1]

With the declaration of war on June 18, 1812, the United States stepped from the profitable sidelines of a global conflict and became a participant. A belligerent nation at last, the United States was neither prepared for war, nor in a position to develop its military quickly. At the war's beginning the American army numbered less than 12,000 men. For a war that was expected largely to be fought on the sea, the United States Navy was also horribly under-armed. There were no ships of the line that could challenge the might of the Royal Navy. There were eight frigates under the American flag, plus a handful of smaller sailing vessels and 170 of President Jefferson's coastal defense gunboats.[2]

Fortunately for the United States, Great Britain was not prepared for the new conflict either. Although the Royal Navy numbered over 600 vessels, with as many as 85 in the Western Hemisphere, it was preoccupied in blockading the European coast, and cruising from the West Indies to the Indian

Ocean, in the ongoing struggle against Napoleon and his allies. It would, therefore, take the Royal Navy some time to reassign and build up the naval force for the war against the United States. On land, with most of the crack troops fighting under Wellington across Spain, British forces were thinly scattered across Canada and in the West Indies. Nor did British military planners know what the American strategy would be.

The Western Theater

As the initiator of war, America—nicknamed Brother Jonathan—struck first. The initial strategy was to mount a four-pronged invasion of Canada in hopes of subduing that colony so Britain would sue for peace. It was only a matter of two weeks before the westernmost arm of the invasion swung into motion. General William Hull, a Connecticut native and a hero of the Revolution, led his militia forces from their base at Detroit across the Detroit River to seize Sandwich (now a section of Windsor), Ontario. But the aging Hull proved no match for Britain's Sir Isaac Brock, who forced a shot-less American surrender and cost the United States control of Detroit and most of the Michigan Territory.

In the fall of the year another American force attempted an invasion 300 miles to the east, along the Niagara River between Lake Erie and Lake Ontario. Here, poorly trained Americans proved no match for the rushing waters of the Niagara River and the well-positioned British forces at Queenston Heights. Although they outnumbered the British better than four to one, American militia faltered in the face of British Iroquois allies. A counterattack drove the Americans back across the river, and 800 were captured. The most important loss for the British was the death of the talented Isaac Brock.

Both of these attempts on Canadian soil were plagued by poor planning, poor leadership, and a lack of discipline. Army commander Henry Dearborn planned to make the major assault on Canada up Lake Champlain to seize Montreal in 1813, but again, ill-trained troops with disorganized leadership failed to secure any success as the British turned back the Americans at Chrysler's Farm along the St. Lawrence River west of Montreal.

The balance of the war in the West depended on who controlled the Great Lakes, most particularly Lake Ontario and Lake Erie—each being a separate theater because Niagara Falls blocked passage between them. Given the dense forests on the frontier between Canada and the United States, moving men and materiel by water was the only practical option. The American strategy for the campaign of 1813 called for taking the British naval bases at Kingston and York (now Toronto) on Lake Ontario. The Yankees could then move on to Forts George and Erie and the northern and southern extremes of the Niagara River. Success in these campaigns would serve as a bargaining chip in peace talks, which the Madison Administration sought while Britain was still engaged in its struggles in Europe.

During 1812, the British—John Bull to the Americans—had dominated Lakes Ontario and Erie with a dozen armed vessels between the two of them. The failures of American arms that year were in large part due to their disadvantage without access to lake transport. Thus, the Americans knew that, come 1813, the lakes must be taken in order to have any success in that theater. Accordingly, in late 1812, Connecticut-born Captain Isaac Chauncey began building up an American naval force that could secure Lakes Ontario and Erie. Chauncey established a base in Lake Erie's Presque Isle, Pennsylvania (later to be known as Erie), and Sackett's Harbor along the New York shore of Lake Ontario.

BATTLE OF LAKE ERIE.—PERRY'S VICTORY.

Rhode Island native Oliver Hazard Perry took command of US forces on Lake Erie early in 1813. He finished outfitting his nine vessels that summer, and on September 10 met the British squadron of six vessels at Put-in-Bay, Ohio. With all of the guns on his flagship *Lawrence* disabled, Commodore Perry took his "Don't Give Up the Ship" pennant and was rowed to the USS *Niagara*. During the balance of the three-hour battle the American carronades pounded the British vessels into surrender. Both sides suffered heavy casualties, but Commodore Perry was able to report, "We have met the enemy and they are ours." As a result of the battle, the US retained control of Lake Erie for the rest of the war. This scrimshaw engraving, inspired by a print, was completed on the whaling bark *Bramin*, ca. 1848.

(© Mystic Seaport Collection, Mystic, CT, #1941.411)

Of course, the British also understood the importance of the American challenge and sought to dominate the lakes through their own shipbuilding program. Chauncey's opposite was the Royal Navy's Sir James Yeo, and the two of them worked diligently through much of 1813 to construct the tonnage they needed to secure the two lakes. What they accomplished was effectual parity. This seemed to fit the disposition of the two leaders, who cautiously parried, but did not seriously risk their warships, or threaten the warships of their opposite. Caution seemed to be the rule of thumb.

A change in approach resulted in a change of command on Lake Erie. That change was linked to an unfortunate incident in Rhode Island waters months before. Rhode Island-born Oliver Hazard Perry had shown his mettle on a number of occasions during the Quasi-War and the Barbary conflicts. He had also been active as commander of *Revenge*, a 70-foot schooner-rigged naval vessel. Before the war, Perry had defended American merchant shipping in *Revenge*, but he lost her on a reef off Watch Hill, Rhode Island, in January of 1811. Though he was exonerated by a court-martial, the energetic Perry was without a command.

The tenor of warfare on Lake Erie changed when Perry was given authority over the theater. Chauncey was only too glad to turn command of Erie over to Perry, declaring that he was "the very person" for the task and "may gain a reputation for Yourself and honour for your country."[3] Perry immediately put his energies to work. In spite of many obstacles, he added nine vessels to the American fleet on Lake Erie. This tipped the balance on the vital waterway, and Perry was quick to press his advantage. On September 10, 1813, the aggressive American closed with the British fleet, now under the command of veteran warrior Robert Barclay. Perry drove his flagship, the new 20-gun brig *Lawrence,* into the British fleet, suffering 80 percent casualties. The *Lawrence* was named in honor of the slain captain of the USS *Chesapeake*, and she flew a flag paraphrasing Lawrence's last words: "Don't Give Up the Ship." With the *Lawrence* disabled, Perry switched his flag to the USS *Niagara* and plunged back into the fray. By the battle's end, Perry was covered in glory. As the American commander noted on his report scrawled on the back of an envelope, "We have met the enemy and they are ours; two ships, two brigs, one schooner and one sloop." So too were the vital waters of Lake Erie.

Perry's victory was quickly followed by an American success on land. Perry's fleet carried William Henry Harrison's western militiamen and regular troops across Lake Erie to attack the retiring British forces in Ontario. Harrison's troops overwhelmed a smaller British and Native-American force in the Battle of the Thames on October 5. During the fall of 1813, the United States had regained all it had lost the previous year, and had established American hegemony in the West that would be challenged, but never be overturned. Of particular import in Harrison's victory at the Thames was the death of the Indian leader Tecumseh. Without his charismatic guidance, the native alliances melted away, as did their hopes of maintaining any control over their territories in the Old Northwest.

The Atlantic Theater

While the war in the west started out badly for the United States, the US Navy on salt water had considerably better luck. Luck perhaps is not the proper term; after all, many US Navy officers were experienced veterans of the Quasi-War or the Barbary conflicts, as were many of their men. The crews were also well disciplined and thoroughly trained. And although the American navy was pathetically small at the war's start with only 17 serviceable fighting vessels, the heart of the small navy was extraordinarily dangerous. Seven frigates served as the core of the US Navy, and the most important of these were the Yankee "super frigates" *Constitution, President,* and *United States.* Rated at 44 guns, they usually carried additional ordnance, and their size and scantlings (dimension of their timbers) were significantly greater than those of their British opponents, which were normally rated at 38 guns or less. Though bigger and stronger, the American super frigates were not slower or less maneuverable than their opponents. Joshua Humphreys's design allowed the American 44s to outrun a British 74-gun ship of the line as well as to run down and defeat a 38-gun frigate.

Luckily these America's capital ships were ready, or nearly ready, for sea when Congress declared war, as was another Humphreys frigate, the 38-gun *Congress.* The Humphreys 38s *Constellation* and *Chesapeake* were in no state to set sail when hostilities began. Several smaller US Navy sloops and brigs of war were in varying states of preparedness. Nonetheless, American commodores and captains pursued a hostile course of action as soon as possible.

Only days after the declaration of war, Commodore John Rodgers departed New York Harbor with a formidable squadron that included the frigates *President, United States,* and *Congress.* Rodgers himself fired the first shot of the war on June 23 when the *President* encountered *HMS Belvidera* southeast of Nantucket. The *President* pursued the smaller frigate, but the *Belvidera* escaped when one of the American cannons exploded, wounding several crewmembers including Rodgers.

Connecticut played an important role in this encounter. *Belvidera* was in southern New England waters in search of the French privateer *Marengo,* which had taken refuge in New London. While in New London, the *Marengo*'s Venetian deckhand Guiseppe Lorenzo went ashore due to illness. With his name Anglicized to Joseph Lawrence he would eventually become one of New London's most important maritime entrepreneurs and public-spirited residents (the city's Lawrence & Memorial Hospital represents a family bequest).[4]

Although the cruise of Commodore Rodgers's squadron yielded only a handful of British merchant ships as prizes, the Americans' aggressive approach was apparent. Then, on July 12 the USS *Constitution* got under way from Chesapeake Bay, bound for New York. Before making port she encountered a British squadron and had to run for sea, at one point using her boats to tow her in the light winds. After three days she escaped and sailed to Boston.

American Sailors in the War of 1812

written by Fred Calabretta

EVEN IN THE BEST of circumstances, the life of a War of 1812 American sailor was one of long absences from home, privation, exhausting toil, strict discipline, and often, exposure to serious danger. For some, the war also brought prison life or the dangers of naval combat.

While the exploits of American naval officers such as Stephen Decatur, Isaac Hull, James Lawrence, Thomas Macdonough, and Oliver Hazard Perry earned them fame and glory and made their names familiar to school children and adults alike, the sailors they commanded remained largely anonymous. Yet, American seamen—especially those of New England—entered the war possessing deep-rooted maritime traditions and skills. These qualities, combined with bravery and a strong sense of duty, helped propel the U.S. Navy to a number of stunning early victories over a British Royal Navy that had long been held in awe for its command of the seas.

When the war began, the American navy consisted of only 16 ships in active service, whereas the British navy had more than 600. Construction of new vessels and conversion of merchant ships soon boosted the size of the fleet and with it the demand for sailors. Naval ships of the period required relatively large crews to handle sails and guns; a 16-gun brig such as the USS *Argus* would have crew of about 125 officers and men, while a 44-gun frigate such as the USS *United States* would carry more than 450 men. When the USS *United States, Macedonian*, and *Hornet* took refuge in the Thames River in 1813, they carried nearly 1,000 men between them.

Service in the U.S. Navy was voluntary, un-like the Royal Navy, which resorted to extensive use of impressment or forced service to fill the crews of a vast fleet. American seamen generally signed on for a two-year term of service. Pay rates ranged from $6.00 per month for boys to $18.00 per month for gunners. A typical seaman earned $10.00 or $12.00 per month. Often, pay advances were offered to entice recruits, as were bounties of $10.00 or $20.00.[1]

The possibility of earning prize money also attracted seamen to the navy's ranks. Captured ships and cargoes were sold at auction, and the U.S. Treasury received 50 percent of the sale price. The balance was divided proportionally among the officers and crew of the ship or ships responsible for the capture. This could be a very lucrative aspect of a sailor's life during the war. In one particularly notable instance, Congress awarded the officers and crew of the frigate *United States* a staggering sum of $200,000 for the capture of HMS *Macedonian*.

The sailors came from all parts of the country, with New England well represented. Many sailors were foreign-born, and a significant number were African-Americans. Detailed regulations shaped their routines and activities. The men were organized into two four-hour watches, which determined their daily schedule and group assignment for handling the ship. Station assignments determined *where* they would perform their duty in all situations, including combat. Berthing and mess assignments established where they would sleep and with whom they would eat.

Organization and order was essential for

John Nugent earned a share of prize money for captured ships and goods during his services on the US Navy brig *Argus*. After her successful cruise in the English Channel in the summer of 1813, the *Argus* was forced to surrender on August 14, 1813, following an engagement with HMS *Pelican*. Casualties on the *Argus* included her captain, who was killed, and Nugent, who suffered a serious leg wound. This document is signed by Connecticut-born Henry Denison (1782-1822), purser on the *Argus*.

(© Mystic Seaport, Denison-Rodgers Collection, Mystic, CT

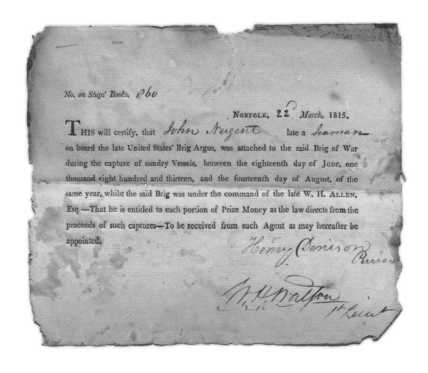

This embroidered sailor's sea bag, created about 1840, features naval scenes and other War of 1812-era images. Throughout the nineteenth century, sea battles inspired many forms of artistic expression, and the resulting creations often represented national pride.

This sea bag has an interesting history of its own, including a 2001 appearance on the popular television program *Antiques Roadshow*.

(© Mystic Seaport Collection, Mystic, CT, #2000.178)

)

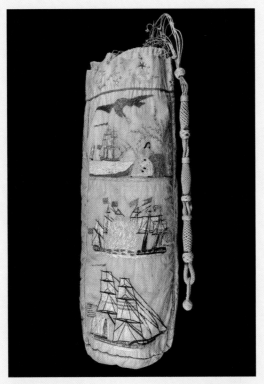

the smooth and effective handling of a ship in all situations. This depended on the performance of her crew. One sailor described a ship as containing "a set of human machinery, in which every man is a wheel, a band, or a crank, all moving with wonderful regularity and precision to the will of its machinist—the all-powerful captain."[2] Performance was maximized and order maintained by the application of strict discipline. Depending on the offense, punishment could be severe, and flogging in front of the assembled ship's company was common.

American sailors were often better trained then their British counterparts. One 1812 veteran recalled typical training: "On one occasion we were at our quarters, exercising in the various evolutions of war; now at our guns, and then going through the forms of boarding the enemy; now running aloft, as if in the act of cutting down our enemy's rigging, and then rushing below, as if to board her, firing our pistols, stabbing with our boarding-pikes, and cutting on all sides with our cutlasses."[3]

Sailors generally wore blue jackets, white trousers, and black hats with brims. Unlike officers, who had bunks, the men slept in hammocks, which were stowed when not in use. Standard American navy rations during the period included salt beef, salt pork, flour, suet, bread (hardtack crackers), cheese, butter, peas, rice, molasses, and vinegar.[4] In terms of volume, salt beef and pork, along with bread, were the most substantial commodities. The men greatly prized an additional ration item—their daily half-pint of grog, which was rum or whiskey diluted with water. Port calls provided opportunities for fresh foods and a varied diet. Live animals were often carried onboard ships for eventual use in the hands of a cook.

In the years leading up to the war, the British navy frequently boarded American merchant ships and wrongfully impressed an estimated 6,000 American seamen.[5] They were taken largely to relieve manpower shortages on British warships then engaged in a long war with France. This activity became a major point of contention between the Great Britain and the United States over freedom of the seas. It could also thrust impressed Americans into dangerous naval battles in a war that was not their own.

At the same time with the frequent desertion of British sailors to American ships, a number of men experienced naval service in *both* navies before and during the War of 1812. This gave them a unique dual perspective on naval life of the period, and they generally seem to have considered life in the American navy as the more desirable of the two.

One such sailor was Samuel Leech, a 14-year-old British sailor serving as a powder monkey in HMS *Macedonian*. He was captured when that ship was forced to surrender following her violent battle with the USS *United States* in October 1812. He subsequently joined the American navy and thus experienced naval life on both sides during the war. He later married and lived for several years in Mansfield and then Somers, Connecticut, before settling in Massachusetts. In the 1840s he wrote a detailed account of his naval career.[6]

Naval life featured an abundance of hazards, including illness, injuries, and accidents such as falls from aloft. In the "age of fighting sail," naval combat represented the ultimate hazard and the defining moment in a sailor's career. Sea battles were characterized by careful ship maneuvering and terrific artillery barrages, and they sometimes culminated in fierce hand-to hand-combat before one of the ships struck her colors. Leech wrote a detailed account of the October 1812 fight between the *Macedonian* and *United States*. Although his description represents the scene on the British ship, it captures in graphic detail the chaos, destruction, and carnage of naval warfare as also experienced by American sailors:

The roaring of cannon could now be heard from all parts of our trembling ship, and, mingling as it did with that of our foes, it made a most hideous noise. By-and-by I heard the shot strike the sides of our ship; the whole scene grew indescribably confused and horrible; it was like some awfully tremendous thunder-storm, whose deafening roar is attended by incessant streaks of lightning, carrying death in every flash, and strewing the ground with the victims of its wrath: only, in our case, the scene was rendered more horrible than that, by the presence of torrents of blood which dyed our decks.

The battle went on. Our men kept cheering with all their might, I cheered with them, though I confess I scarcely knew for what. . . . Such was the terrible scene, amid which we kept on our shouting and firing … the din of battle continued. Grape and canister shot were pouring through our portholes like leaden rain, carrying death in their trail. The large shot came against the ship's side like iron hail, shaking her to the very keel, or passing through her timbers, and scattering terrific splinters, which did a more appalling work than even their own death-giving blows. . . . Suddenly, the rattling of the iron hail ceased. We were ordered to cease firing … we were in the state of a complete wreck.[7]

Although the War of 1812 ranks small in scale compared to a number of other American wars, it resulted in the death or wounding of more than 700 members of the U.S. Navy.[8]

The U.S. Navy emerged from the War of 1812 with a lofty image and a place of high esteem in the hearts of most Americans. Although individual officers received much of the glory and acclaim, the sailors too were greatly admired. Along with their ships, the men of the U.S. Navy acquired a heroic stature, representing—in public perception—the best of patriotism, courage, fortitude, and honor that America had to offer. Their experiences inspired poetry, songs, plays, and art. Through their exploits during the War of 1812, sailors established themselves as iconic representatives of America.

This deck scene depicts gun crews cheering with enthusiasm and standing ready for action as the USS *Constitution* prepares to do battle with HMS *Guerriere*. US Navy sailors were both seamen, who stood watch and handled sails, and members of small fighting teams who operated the cannons and prepared to board an enemy ship and fight hand-to-hand with cutlass and pistol. Published in *Ballou's Pictorial Drawing Room Companion* in 1851, this wood engraving by John Andrew mirrors enduring popular perceptions of the courage and fighting spirit of American sailors.
(© Mystic Seaport Collection, Mystic, CT, #1939.7)

The *Constitution* left Boston in early August in search of British frigates to challenge. She was commanded by Captain Isaac Hull, a native of Derby, Connecticut, who had first established his reputation as a fighting officer during the Quasi-War. His executive officer was Charles Morris of landlocked Woodstock, Connecticut, whose fighting experience was similar.

South of Nova Scotia the *Constitution* sighted HMS *Guerriere*, a 38-gun frigate commanded by the brave British Captain Richard Dacres. As the ships closed for action the *Constitution*'s superior gunnery toppled two of the *Guerriere*'s masts within 15 minutes and defeated her within the hour. The shattered British frigate could not be salvaged, but the *Constitution*'s damage was very slight. The sight of British cannonballs bouncing off her sides earned her the nickname "Old Ironsides" during this engagement.

Following the path of his seafaring father, Isaac Hull (1773-1843) left his home in Derby, Connecticut, at the age of 14 to join the merchant service, sailing out of New London at least once. He joined the US Navy in 1798 and moved rapidly up through the ranks during the Quasi-War with France and the Barbary War. His success earned him command of the USS *Constitution* in 1810 (which wintered at New London in 1810-11). In August 1812 he commanded her during the battle with HMS *Guerriere*, the US Navy's first significant victory at sea during the war, which won fame for Hull and the nickname "Old Ironsides" for his ship. Hull served ashore through the rest of the war, and for much of the rest of his long naval career, but his name and portrait were well known in countless American homes.

(© Mystic Seaport Collection, Mystic, CT, #1961.694)

Taking the war to European waters, the USS *United States*, under the command of Stephen Decatur, vanquished HMS *Macedonian* in October. This second American ship-to-ship victory was followed in late December by another *Constitution* success. Captain William Bainbridge, who outranked Hull, took the *Constitution* and the 20-gun sloop of war *Hornet* south to interdict British shipping routes off Brazil, and he encountered HMS *Java* on December 29. Although the *Constitution* suffered damage during the three-hour battle, the *Java* was dismasted and forced to surrender. The *Java* was such a wreck that she was determined to by worthless, and so was burned at sea.[5]

These and other early victories by the 18-gun sloop of war *Wasp* over HMS *Frolic* in October 1812—though the *Wasp* was immediately captured herself—and by the *Hornet* over HMS *Peacock* in a 15-minute fight in February 1813 proved a big embarrassment to the Royal Navy and a big boost to American morale.

For every action there is a reaction, which in wartime is often not equal. Just as the American Congress was authorizing construction of three US 74-gun ships of the line—which would not be ready until 1814—the British began to strengthen the Royal Navy's presence along the American coast and in the Caribbean in order to overwhelm Brother Jonathan's upstart navy. In early 1813, the number of British warships in the theater increased to an even 100, including 10 74-gun ships of the line and 38 frigates. Over the following months, the British blockade extended north from the border with Spanish Florida to include the whole American coast, except that of New England. British strategy allowed New England to remain largely untouched in order to encourage the region to continue its protests against the war, and to allow Yankee ships to carry provisions to British (spell that e-n-e-m-y) possessions in Canada and the West Indies.[6]

The British blockade of American ports expanded and tightened throughout 1813. In doing so, it collapsed the young republic's foreign trade, bringing an end all together to the period of boom

and bust that had begun back in 1793. Even the coasting trade was choked nearly to death by the weight of British iron. The American economy suffered as a result, with shortages in some areas, gluts in others and financial speculation that endangered the nation even more.[7]

At sea, 1813 saw mixed results between the belligerent navies. In January, the 12-gun US brig *Viper* was overwhelmed by the British frigate *Narcissus* off Central America. In February, the 46-gun USS *Essex*, which had been built by public subscription in Massachusetts in 1799, rounded Cape Horn to attack the British whaling fleet in the Pacific. She was the first US Navy ship to enter the Pacific Ocean, and in the spring of 1813 she captured about 15 British whaleships. On June 1, the bold British Captain Philip Broke of the 38-gun HMS *Shannon*, which was blockading Boston, issued a challenge to Captain James Lawrence of the 38-gun USS *Chesapeake* (actually carrying 50 guns). The *Chesapeake* was already bound out to sea, flying a pennant proclaiming "Free Trade and Sailors' Rights." The *Chesapeake*'s approach maneuver failed, and the well-drilled crew of the *Shannon* raked her, then closed for the kill. Mortally wounded, Lawrence exhorted his crew something along the lines of "Don't give up the ship!" as he was carried below. But the ship was given up within 15 minutes.

That summer, the 18-gun brig of war *Argus* delivered a new US minister to France to replace Connecticut-born Ambassador Joel Barlow, who had died in Poland while following Napoleon to Russia to get confirmation of France's stand with the US. The *Argus* then cruised against British commerce in the English Channel, only to be outmaneuvered and defeated by HMS *Pelican* in a 45-minute battle on August 14. Three weeks later, off the coast of Maine, the 16-gun US Brig *Enterprise* took the 14-gun Royal Navy brig *Boxer* in a 30-minute fight that claimed the lives of both captains.

Connecticut Privateers

written by Andrew W. German

THE PRIVATEERSMEN, may they receive reasonable encouragement from Congress as they hazard their lives, for small profits, while they render an essential service to our government"

— TOAST BY DR. VINE UTLEY,
SURGEON OF THE NEW LONDON
PRIVATEER *MARS*, 1812-13

President James Madison did not intend to employ merchant mariners as maritime warriors in the impending new war with Great Britain, but only eight days after voting to declare war, Congress passed the Act Concerning Letters of Marque, which authorized the secretary of state to license private armed vessels. The concept of privately owned armed vessels waging war went back at least as far as the 1100s among the Italian city states. By 1400, letters of reprisal permitted preying on enemy vessels in one's territorial waters, and letters of marque licensed attacks in foreign waters. Privateers—private vessels armed specifically to capture the enemy's merchant ships—and trading vessels carrying letters-of marque and reprisal authorizing them to capture enemy vessels during their regular trading voyages, had played a large role during the Revolutionary War at sea. A mixture of veteran privateersmen and aggressive young captains hoped to be equally effective during this second British war.[1]

To distinguish privateering from piracy, strict rules were devised through the centuries. During the War of 1812, the State Department sent printed commissions signed by the president to local customs collectors for issue to captains, who posted performance bonds. Privateers could board vessels on the high seas but not in neutral waters. Enemy vessels, or enemy goods on neutral vessels, could be seized and sent to an American or allied port for sale. Generally at least one enemy crewmember was sent in to give testimony to a prize commissioner to verify that the capture was legal. If a prize court approved the seizure, the vessel and cargo were sold at auction and the proceeds were divided among the shareholders and crew, with any required duties deducted, along with 2 percent of the value to be contributed to the fund for disabled seamen.[2]

The war's first privateers were converted merchant vessels. The 56-foot Guilford sloop *Actress*, commanded by Captain G. Lumden, may have been the first Connecticut privateer, getting to sea on July 11, followed two weeks later by the Stonington schooner *Lewis*, commanded by Benjamin Pendleton. Both vessels survived about a week before being captured by the Royal Navy.[3]

By the fall of 1812, the first generation of vessels built specifically as privateers went to sea. Late in September, Captain Oliver Champlain of New London obtained a commission for his brand-new schooner *Joel Barlow*. Named in honor of the Connecticut-born poet and minister to France, she was built in East Hartford and carried eight cannons and a crew of 90. Champlain headed south in October to harass the British West Indies shipping lanes. The *Barlow* captured several

To Captain   commander of the private armed

called the

INSTRUCTIONS

FOR THE PRIVATE ARMED VESSELS OF THE UNITED STATES,

1. THE tenor of your commission under the act of Congress, entitled " An act concerning letters of marque, prizes, and prize goods," a copy of which is hereto annexed, will be kept constantly in your view. The high seas, referred to in your commission, you will understand, generally, to extend to low water mark ; but with the exception of the space within one league, or three miles, from the shore of countries at peace both with Great Britain and with the United States. You may nevertheless execute your commission within that distance of the shore of a nation at war with Great Britain, and even on the waters within the jurisdiction of such nation, if permitted so to do.

2. You are to pay the strictest regard to the rights of neutral powers, and the usages of civilized nations ; and in all your proceedings towards neutral vessels, you are to give them as little molestation or interruption as will consist with the right of ascertaining their neutral character, and of detaining and bringing them in for regular adjudication, in the proper cases. You are particularly to avoid even the appearance of using force or seduction, with a view to deprive such vessels of their crews, or of their passengers, other than persons in the military service of the enemy.

3. Towards enemy vessels and their crews, you are to proceed, in exercising the rights of war, with all the justice and humanity which characterize the nation of which you are members.

4. The master and one or more of the principal persons belonging to captured vessels, are to be sent, as soon after the capture as may be, to the judge or judges of the proper court in the United States, to be examined upon oath, touching the interest or property of the captured vessel and her lading : and at the same time are to be delivered to the judge or judges, all passes, charter parties, bills of lading, invoices, letters and other documents and writings found on board ; the said papers to be proved by the affidavit of the commander of the capturing vessel, or some other person present at the capture, to be produced as they were received, without fraud, addition, subduction or embezzlement.

By command of the President of the U. States of America.

Jas Monroe   *Secretary of State.*

This document signed by Secretary of State, and future president, James Monroe, lists the instructions to privateer captains prescribed by the Congressional Act Concerning Letters of Marque, Prizes and Prize Goods. When the New London privateer *Mars* arrived off the Azores on December 11, 1812, according to Surgeon Vine Utley, "We hove too, Dined, and then the Commander called his counsel of officers, His Clerk read the laws of Congress relative to present privateering business, instructions &c. from the Secretary of War."

(Document, © Mystic Seaport Collection, Mystic, CT; quote, Rhode Island Historical Society, MSS 828, Box 12, Folder 8)

When Captain Charles Bulkeley advertised in the *Connecticut Gazette* on October 13, 1812, seeking crew members for his privateer *Mars*, he emphasized the two aspects of privateering: patriotism and profits.

(New London County Historical Society; Photographer: Dennis Murphy)

NOTICE.

To young able-bodied Mariners, who are desirous to serve their country and make their Fortunes.

THE Schooner Privateer MARS, built on the latest and most approved construction, both for convenience and sailing, is now fitting, and will be ready to sail on a Cruise soon. Please to apply to CHARLES BULKELEY, on board said Schooner.
New-London, Oct. 13.

Mrs. Sally Stockman,

prizes and took British merchandise out of a Spanish vessel before returning to New London in December. Her second cruise, beginning in January 1813, ended in Charleston.[4]

A celebrated veteran of Revolutionary War privateering, New London's Captain Charles Bulkeley, age 59, commissioned a privateer schooner with the warlike name *Mars*. She was "built upon the new and most improved plan for fast sailing"—meaning designed on the Baltimore or Chesapeake Bay pilot model, with long, narrow hull, low freeboard, and very tall rig. "She carries a cloud of canvass, and dances over the waves like a feather," remarked her surgeon, Vine Utley, whose journal, offering many details of privateer operation, is quoted here. She mounted one swiveling 24-pound "long Tom" and eight 6-pound cannon. Her crew of 93 included five prize masters who would take command of captured vessels. Her owners represented New London, Groton, Norwich, and Hartford.[5]

The *Mars* departed New London on November 17, 1812, bound for the trade routes in the eastern Atlantic. A very stormy passage brought them to the Azores on December 3, and they next day they took their first prize "without our being oblige to fire a single gun, even to bring him too."

The *Mars* took three more vessels, and on Christmas eve: "We gave chase to one, and came within cannon shot by 9 o'clock A.M. and gave her 3 shots from the 24 pounder, . . . We soon found her to be an armed vessel by her commencing a fire upon us. . . . A scattering fire was kept up about half an hour, at which time we came near enough to fire grape shot about their ears, upon which she soon struck her proud colours to us."

Although Captain Bulkeley made the command decisions, he did consult with his officers and prize masters, several of whom owned shares in the *Mars*. After such a consultation on December 29, with six prizes taken, they decided "for the interests of the owners and crew of the Mars to cruise along towards Madeira, the coasts of Spain, the Canary Islands and from thence homeward to the United States."

On New Year's Day, "We drank freely of sour punch at 11 o'clock, dined on good animal food & an excellent plumb pudding, after dinner we drank a glass of sherry wine, which we had lately won by our adventures, and wished each other a happy new year."

The next day the lookout at the masthead sighted a sail. "Our men by labouring hard at the sweeps [14 long oars, operated by 70 men] without intermission brought us within cannon shot of the vessel about an hour before the setting of the sun. We gave her a shot from the long Tom." Finally, in the waning light, Captain Bulkeley raised his speaking trumpet and ordered the British captain to "come on board

the Mars in his own boat, which order he immediately complied with."

So another prize was taken, which added to the prisoners under guard in the hold. Sentries paced the deck and called out every half hour during the night, but on January 17 they discovered the prisoners using a file to remove their shackles so they could seize the *Mars*. The next day she took another prize, and Captain Bulkeley made it a cartel vessel to carry 25 paroled captives to England.

With 11 prizes taken, food and water running short, and the wet and moldy quarters making the crew sick, Captain Bulkeley turned toward home. But Atlantic winter gales repeatedly threatened the *Mars*, driving her away from her destination and testing the endurance of her crew. Struggling past the Gulf Stream, the sleek vessel nearly met with catastrophe, when, "Just as we had cleared the cabin of water, another heavy sea rolled onto our decks and buried her in water six feet deep." Though nearly filled with water, the *Mars* rose after two desperate minutes to continue toward home with her battered and shaken crew.

At last, on February 25, 1813, Utley wrote: "Every man was flushed with joy at the sight of his Native shore. We all rose early, & as soon as the day dawned with sails unfurled we seized the favourable gale from the S.W and ran up into New London Harbor, where we arrived about the middle of the day. As we passed Fort Trumbull with colors flying we fired eleven guns, one gun for each prize, which were answered from the garrison. As soon as we cast Ankor, which was off in the channel of the harbor, the wharfs were soon crouded with the people of the city, who gave us three welcome cheers while we were droping the Ankers which resounded thro the harbor and struck my ear with pleasure, to hear the voice of my Native Citizens once more."

Two prizes eventually found their way to New London, but the rest remained unreported.

While awaiting word of the missing prizes and his prize-master son, Captain Bulkeley solicited crew for a second voyage, offering a $20 bounty. But before he could get under way, Commodore Decatur's squadron arrived and the Royal Navy sealed the port, ending the career of the privateer *Mars*.[6]

The record for the shortest successful privateering voyage is undoubtedly held by the little sloop *Hero* of Mystic. A 13-year-old coasting sloop, she had already been captured once and ransomed on a passage from Charleston to Mystic. After HMS *Ramillies* captured the Mystic sloop *Fox* at the beginning of April 1813 and armed her as a British cruiser, a number of Mystic mariners decided to recapture her. Captain Ambrose Burrows gathered 30 volunteers and one cannon on April 13 and sailed to New London, where he obtained a letter of marque. The *Hero* departed at 2:00 p.m. the next day, convoying several coasting schooners as far as Watch Hill before heading for Block Island. At 5:00 p.m. they sighted the *Fox* several miles southeast of the island, and an hour later she turned, intending to capture the *Hero*. The sloops came together at 7:00, and the *Hero*'s crew overwhelmed the 13 men on the *Fox* without firing a shot. The two vessels arrived in Mystic at 11:30 p.m., having made a successful privateering voyage of nine and a half hours.[7]

With the British squadron off New London and patrolling the Sound, Connecticut ports did not commission seagoing privateers after the spring of 1813. However, the increasing number of Connecticut residents willing to load their boats with goods and trade with Royal Navy ships gave rise to a new form of privateer, the private armed boat. Perhaps inspired by the British barges that overtook and captured so many coasting vessels, at least eight of them were commissioned in New London. Daniel Ladd's *Experiment*, a 36-foot boat powered by 20 oars, raced up the Sound as far as Milford in December 1813, capturing one suspicious boat.

The most successful private armed boats were the *Yankee* and *True Blooded Yankee* of Mystic. Lemuel Burrows's *Yankee* prowled the Sound and even seized former British consul James Stewart at Plum Island in September 1814. The *True Blooded Yankee* went as far as Massachusetts waters, where she captured a sloop with provisions for the British.[8]

The Hartford-owned schooner *Blockade*, commanded by John Mix, and the Middletown-built *Anaconda*, commanded by Nathaniel Shaler of Bridgeport, had mixed success sailing out of New York. Stratford's Samuel Nicoll was very successful with the New York privateer *Scourge*, and both New Londoner Guy R. Champlin and Norwich native Samuel Chester Reid had notable voyages with the New York schooner *General Armstrong*. Milford's George Coggeshall and Adam Pond carried letters of marque during their trading voyages in the Milford-built schooners *David Porter* and *Sine qua non*. Commanding the *Governor Tompkins* in 1813, Nathaniel Shaler engaged a British frigate. He later reported on two black sailors who were mortally wounded. One asked to be thrown overboard so he didn't impede the crew, while John Johnson, with his body torn open by a cannonball, called out, "Fire away my boys!— No haul a color down." Shaler concluded, "Whilst America has such tars, she has little to fear from European tyrants."[9]

Exciting stories aside, the purpose of privateering was to profit by disrupting the enemy's trade. The premier privateering port of Baltimore has received the most analysis, and the data indicate that of the port's 126 privateers, 54 (43 percent) took prizes during their cruises, while 57 percent of the privateers failed to make a capture. The financial risk was almost matched by the danger of destruction: 43 percent of Baltimore's privateers were lost, with 40 captured, 8 chased ashore, and 6 lost at sea. Overall, of 515 American letter-of-marque vessels, 300 (58 percent) failed to make a capture, and 250 (49 percent) were taken by the British—a percentage matched by Connecticut-owned or -commanded vessels. A few were spectacularly successful. The Baltimore schooner *Surprise* took a likely record 43 prizes. The average take for successful vessels was 11—the total taken by Captain Bulkeley's *Mars*.[10]

But the resolution of the *Mars* captures emphasizes the marginal profits in privateering. She took 11 prizes during her 100-day voyage and sent 9 of them home. Only three arrived. Captain Bulkeley's son Thomas and his prize crew were lost at sea, as were Prize Master Rufus Avery of Groton and his crew. The others were recaptured at sea, representing the loss of 27 of the *Mars*'s 93 crewmembers and two-thirds of her potential profits. The prize vessels and cargoes were auctioned for approximately $25,000. When duties and fees were deducted, each of the 153-1/8 shares in the 100-day voyage was worth about $140.[11]

As for disrupting the trade of Great Britain, privateers did capture an estimated 1,300 British merchant vessels overall, nearly 400 of them in the first year of the war. But when measured against the overall volume of trade, those losses amounted to less than 5 percent of the British merchant marine and were easily sustainable. And the Royal Navy was large enough to protect the merchant marine. In May of 1813, three British warships safely conducted a convoy of 226 merchant ships from the West Indies to England. Privateers did, however, increase the risk and uncertainty of shipping for British merchants, with insurance rates rising as much as 13 percent. This led to loud cries by influential British merchants for a speedy resolution to the war. In the end, the privateers' greatest value was the threat they posed, rather than the actual damage inflicted by the republic's private navy.[12]

Thomas Masterman Hardy (1769-1839) first joined the Royal Navy at age 12. Proving himself a brave and capable officer, Hardy was promoted to captain of Admiral Horatio Nelson's flagship in 1798. Hardy commanded Nelson's HMS *Victory*, and attended to the mortally wounded Nelson, when the British fleet defeated the combined French and Spanish fleet at the Battle of Trafalgar in October 1805. Made a baronet in 1806, Hardy took command of HMS *Ramillies* in 1812 and remained in her through the War of 1812, serving off New London almost continuously from April 1813 to August 1814. After the war, he commanded at sea until 1827 and was promoted to rear admiral in 1825.

This steel engraving by H. Robinson is based on an 1834 portrait by Robert Evans.

(New London County Historical Society, 2012.10.01)

While American and British warships exchanged shots in the Atlantic, and private armed vessels attempted to profit by plundering the enemy's merchant vessels, the Royal Navy tightened its grip on the US coast. Admiral George Cockburn roamed freely from Delaware Bay to Chesapeake Bay. In early April he bombarded Lewes, Delaware, employing Congreve rockets for the first time in the war. Three weeks later he sailed up Chesapeake Bay and attacked the Principio iron furnace, which produced cannons, and burned the small Maryland ports of Frenchtown, Havre de Grace, Georgetown, and Fredericktown. An unsuccessful attempt to seize the Gosport Navy Yard and USS *Constellation* at Norfolk in June was followed by the invasion of Hampton, Virginia, across Hampton Roads from Norfolk, where rape, murder, and pillage were reported. Throughout much of the summer and into the fall, the Chesapeake suffered at the hands of the wide-ranging British naval forces. They penetrated up the Rappahannock River, attacked islands scattered around the bay, and fired on communities, taking aim on St. Michaels, Maryland, on August 10.

Even as the Royal Navy ranged the coves and inlets behind the Virginia Capes in 1813, it became a regular presence in waters bordering Connecticut. British warships had patrolled the area since the summer of 1812, occasionally overhauling a merchant vessel. But in the spring of 1813 a small squadron settled in. One April 14, 1813, New London's weekly newspaper, the *Connecticut Gazette* reported: "The British Standard is erected on Block-Island; and a wharf is building for the convenience of landing from the fleet. Fresh meat and good water is procured on the Island sufficient for the supply of the enemy's ships."[8]

The squadron was commanded by Captain Sir Thomas Masterman Hardy of HMS *Ramillies*, a 74-gun ship of the line. Hardy's reputation as Admiral Lord Horatio Nelson's favorite, and captain of HMS *Victory* when Nelson died in his arms at Trafalgar, was known and respected in America. As he settled in to this new station, he told some detained merchant captains, "it being my wish as much as possible to soften the hardships of individuals during this very unpleasant, and I sincerely hope short, hostility between the two countries." Hardy was quite amenable to releasing an impressed American seaman from his ship, and when news of Admiral Cockburn's depredations reached New London the newspaper reported that Commodore Hardy "has repeatedly asserted that he is only making war against commerce and armed ships. He has expressed a detestation of the burning and marauding system. If the term is admissible, he is an honorable enemy."[9]

Things changed abruptly when Commodore Stephen Decatur's squadron arrived in local waters. As master of the USS *United States*, he led a squadron that included her captive, now USS *Macedonian*, and the sloop of war *Hornet*. These two vessels were commanded by former officers of the USS *Wasp*, Jacob Jones and James Biddle. Decatur attempted to break through the British blockade of

New York, but the weather turned against them and they left by way of Long Island Sound. After several days inside Fishers Island, on June 1—the day HMS *Shannon* defeated USS *Chesapeake*—the squadron broke for the open sea off Block Island. But as British ships converged, Decatur ordered a return to the safety of New London Harbor. Suddenly Hardy had to put the plug in a very volatile bottle.

"You will learn of Decaturs Squadron having been chased into this harbor by the Ramillies and the Orpheus, which has caused great alarm in this place, & has induced every person to move their property out of the city except myself," wrote former British consul James Stewart on June 4. "I believe the Blockading Squadron will come in after the frigates & every preparation is making to oppose them by building forts &c &c &c & about 2000 of the militia have come in."[10]

Militiaman Samuel Goodrich, of Ridgefield, Connecticut, was one month short of his 20th birthday when he arrived on June 8. With "cocked hats, long tailed blue coats . . . and cutlasses by our side," Goodrich and his fellow artillerists made "a fine company," while their "glittering cannon moved along with the solemnity of elephants." As the men and women of the threatened seaport expressed their appreciation, "louder screamed our fife, deeper rolled our drum, and the . . . music echoed and reechoed from the reverberating walls of the street. It was a glorious thing to belong to such a company." But Goodrich also observed the "black and portentous squadron" afloat at the harbor's mouth. "They seemed very near at hand, and for the first time I realized my situation—that of a soldier, who was likely soon to be engaged in battle."

Assigned to the outer defenses of Groton's Fort Griswold, he and his company settled into a routine. This included, of course, drilling, standing guard, taking a turn as part of the unit's three-man fishing crew that supplied fresh fish from the river each day, and marching to church each Sunday in full military regalia. While carrying dispatches for his company commander to New London and to Decatur's squadron upriver near Gales Ferry, Goodrich met the celebrated Mrs. Anna Bailey—known in Groton Bank for volunteering her flannel petticoat as cannon wadding during an early alarm at Fort Griswold—who was filled with a "most peppery essence." When they delivered a message to the advanced post at Avery Point, Goodrich and his companion suffered a short bombardment from the frigate *Acasta*. Sheltered behind some rocks, they "could trace the cannon-balls as they flew by looking like globes of mist, twinkling through the air. . . . the noise they made, as they rose high in the air, was a strange mixture between a howl and a scream."

Goodrich's most trying moment came during picket duty on a night when the militia on both sides of the river expected imminent attack from the enlarged British squadron. He reported years later that, "the sounds on all sides were at last hushed, and left the world to darkness, and to me." Out in the black night he knew were friends and enemies, armed and on edge. Eventually he

Captain Stephen Decatur (1779-1820) achieved naval prominence following his bold and successful actions during the Barbary War, 1801-05. During the first year of the War of 1812, he commanded the USS *United States* when she captured HMS *Macedonian.* On June 1, 1813, Decatur's three-ship squadron was chased into New London Harbor by ships of the British blockading force. Failing at several unconventional efforts to break free of the blockade, Decatur laid up his ships and departed from Connecticut in May 1814. Taking command of the USS *President,* Decatur was captured in January 1815 trying to escape from New York. The British returned Captain Decatur to New London in time to participate in the peace ball there. Decatur was killed in a duel with fellow naval officer James Barron in 1820.

(© Mystic Seaport Collection, Mystic, CT, #1952.213)

This watercolor painting, *Fort Trumbull as Rebuilt in 1813*, depicts a New London fort that has changed significantly over time. The first defensive works on this site were established during the Revolutionary War and named for then-governor John Trumbull. During the War of 1812 it was principally manned by a contingent of regular US artillerymen. In June 1813, Governor John Cotton Smith described Fort Trumbull as a "mere water battery, mounting 22 guns, manned by about seventy raw recruits commanded by an officer of spirit no doubt but without experience; its magazine liable to be blown up by the first shell that shall enter the garrison." Today, New London visitors may tour the site of Fort Trumbull, now home to an imposing stone fort constructed from 1839 to 1852.

(New London Maritime Society, Howard Collection)

heard the dipping of oars and the slapping of waves against the prow of a boat. His challenge "echoed portentously in the silence, but no answer was given, and the low, black, raking apparition glided on its way." Another challenge went unanswered, and "on went the ghost." He cocked his gun, and "the click sounded ominously in the still night air." Then he "began to consider the horror of shooting some fellow-being in the dark." Finally the "rudder was turned, the boat whirled on her heel," and Goodrich found himself confronted with a local fisherman. Off to the guardhouse they went. "So," Goodrich reported, "I can boast that I made one prisoner."

Samuel Goodrich's service in Groton lasted for six weeks. He recalled that "a general reading of bad books, a great deal of petty gambling, and not a little tippling" characterized life in the encampment. Goodrich returned to his home aware that "corrupting influences" took their toll on young men "exposed to new and unexpected seductions." Yet, Goodrich would look back on his service with pleasure, reporting four decades later that "there were feelings of fraternity established between members of the company which have continued to this day."[11]

Hardy moved his squadron closer and cracked down further, especially after local mariners instituted a guerrilla war, as described in the next chapter. A month later *Niles' Register* could cite Hardy's assertion "that he was determined to punish the coasters, and *learn them* TO VOTE *differently*, and turn out the present administration. This is warm electioneering." On June 13, the *Gazette* reported several vessels taken and burned at the mouth of the Connecticut River, and the same day a small schooner was cut out of the Mystic River. "It appears certain that every thing which floats, that falls into the hands of the enemy, not worth keeping, will be destroyed. The fishermen should stay at home." Two weeks later, four armed British barges chased two small vessels as far as the Connecticut River lighthouse and fired into the town of Saybrook. "Long shot were thrown from the barges among our dwelling houses," complained the residents.[12]

July 12 was a day to remember in New London. As described by Sylvanus Griswold of

Connecticut's Militia

written by Fred Calabretta

AT A TIME WHEN THE NATIONS in Europe are all in arms against each other and are spreading death and destruction, and at a time when our country is threatened with the same calamity, the United States have no other means than this militia, we are the great bulwark against a foreign invasion. It is to us all will look for security; our wives, our children will depend on us for protection, in which we are determined they shall not be disappointed.

The officers and soldiers of the 3rd Brigade will never lack ambition and pride to prompt them to do their duty while they reflect that they are Americans, and that the price of the liberty we now enjoy was the blood of our fathers, and that same spirit which so gloriously achieved our liberty can and will defend it against the attack and violence of all foreign powers, that the ideas be a stimulus to every officer and soldier to do his duty and thoroughly requaint himself with military discipline.

Let us bear in mind that our great Washington told us that if we wished to preserve peace we ought at all time be prepared for war.

WILLIAM WILLIAMS,
BRIGADIER GENERAL
CONNECTICUT STATE MILITIA
AUGUST 31, 1807[1]

General Williams, in an attempt to inspire his men, effectively characterized the heritage and responsibilities of the state's citizen soldiers and articulated the serious expectations incumbent on them and their service. When the War of 1812 began, few other states could claim a militia that was better prepared and equipped. But few states would see the power of their militia so closely husbanded as that of Connecticut.

State militias were designed to provide a means of defense in time of need while reducing the necessity of a large standing army. Maintaining standing armies was a costly matter. They were also viewed as a threat since they could conceivably be used to strengthen a tyrant at the expense of the peoples' liberties. This was an understandable concern in the decades of the late eighteenth and early nineteenth centuries—a period characterized by revolution against arbitrary power.

Connecticut's militia traditions, modeled after practices in England, dated back to the early colonial period. In the early decades of the colony's existence, Connecticut men participated in the ongoing power struggle in North America that pitted English colonists against Native Americans, and later against the French.

Connecticut first asserted sole authority for its own militia during King William's War, which was fought from 1689 to 1698. When the King of England authorized the governor of New York to command militia units from other colonies, he attempted to exercise his control over the Connecticut militia. The people of Connecticut protested to King William, citing their chartered right to control their own militia. The king ultimately rescinded the New York governor's authority. A precedent had been set, and with the outbreak of the War of 1812,

Connecticut would once again steadfastly stand by her right to command her own troops.

The colony refined the structure of its militia with an act "for better regulating the militia" issued in 1739.[2] This act provided a basic framework that would remain in place for over 100 years. The act outlined the command structure, with the governor at the top. It established 13 regiments combining town militia companies by region. Regiments were in turn grouped into brigades.

After the American Revolution (during which the militia was intermittently called up for service), Connecticut and the other states also complied, in varying degrees, with the federal government's Uniform Militia Act of 1792. This act stipulated that all able-bodied white male citizens between the ages of 18 and 45 were required to enroll in the militia unless otherwise exempt for some specific reason such as serious health issues. Militiamen were required to supply their own arms and equipment. Militia companies were formed in each town, although smaller towns would often merge their forces to achieve the desired complement of men. A few companies of artillery and cavalry were included in the state militia structure. State law required militia companies to report or "muster" for training and inspection at regular intervals, usually four times per year.

Each company was to consist of 64 privates, although in actual practice the number varied. Lower-ranking officers were elected annually by the men of each militia company, while the higher ranks were filled by men appointed by the state. Their service was a badge of pride and frequently a pathway to political office as well.

Connecticut's comprehensive militia laws were sophisticated enough to anticipate an issue that continues to be relevant today. They accommodated anti-war religious beliefs by providing exemptions for members of the "Societies of Friends, Shakers and Quakers."[3] Instead of military service, these individuals were required to pay a fee of ten dollars annually to the state treasurer. Monies collected for these exemptions, as well as other militia-related fines and fees, contributed significantly to the state treasury.

The principal arm of each militia member was a flintlock musket. These muzzle-loading weapons fired a round ball and were highly inaccurate, except at close range. They were often of New England manufacture, and some were produced in Connecticut by arms-makers such as Eli Whitney. When reporting for active duty, the men were expected to possess 20 cartridges and two extra flints.

By 1800, most of Connecticut had long ceased to be a wild frontier. As a result, and despite militia training, many of the men in the state had very limited experience with firearms and artillery fieldpieces. This lack of familiarity led to numerous accidents and serious injuries, often during training exercises. State records for the period leading up to the War of 1812 include a number of petitions seeking compensation for such injuries, which generally resulted from burst muskets and the accidental discharge of fieldpieces.[4]

When the War of 1812 began, few states could claim militias that were better prepared for service than that of Connecticut. However, *philosophically*, the militiamen, state leaders, and the general population were not at all ready for the men to serve, largely in response to several key federal actions.

On June 12, 1812, a week before the declaration of war, General Henry Dearborn, senior general in command of forces in the Northeast, ordered five companies of Connecticut militia to New London and New Haven for the defense of those coastal cities. They were to be placed under the command of federal officers.

Governor Roger Griswold and his council addressed two key issues in considering their response. Could the Connecticut militia be called out if the specific contingencies stated in the U.S. Constitution did not apply, and could it be commanded by federal officers? Connecticut's leaders pointed out that the Constitution authorized Congress to call out the militia "to execute the laws of the union, suppress insurrections and repel invasion" and that no such conditions existed. They also noted that the Constitution assured militia units the right to serve under their own officers. This traditional and highly valued practice of leadership by men of their own choosing became a major point of contention, as it had been more than 100 years earlier.

Connecticut and several sister states strongly protested the US government's request that state troops enter federal service. Citing the state's rights under the Constitution, Connecticut refused the federal request, and Governor Griswold issued a proclamation to that effect on August 6, 1812. Ultimately, the state did provide a force for federal service with volunteers drawn from militia units. This created what was essentially a special state army referred to as the State Corps or State Military Corps. This transfer of men reduced many militia companies to a typical strength of 30 to 40 men.[5] In an interesting arrangement, the State Corps, while in service to and supplied by the US government, was under the command of Major General William Williams of the state militia. Connecticut steadfastly continued to stand by her right to command her own troops.

Although the militia would ultimately be called into service to protect the state's coast, Connecticut had again exercised her rights pertaining to the militia, the *Hartford Courant* echoed the popular response to this decision: "Let our militia rally around the state government, to which they are indebted for not being called out to jeopardize their lives garrisoning our forts; to which they are indebted for not being dragged out of state to fight Indians or die before the walls of Quebec."[6]

Beginning in 1812, Connecticut updated several of its militia laws. It revised uniform regulations in a General Order issued in February 1812, setting a standard for how militiamen would be clothed during the war. Privates were to wear blue coats lined with white and trimmed with red, with white buttons and standup collars. Also specified were white woolen vests, blue woolen pants, and hats with a common crown and the brim turned up on the left side. The designated footwear was bootees or half-boots. The requirements and colors varied slightly for the artillery, cavalry, and musicians. Officers were to be similarly attired, with the addition of long-skirted coats and "modern military hats."[7] In practice, standard uniforms were often in short supply. The men tended to wear clothing that was on hand or uniforms created from any fabric, buttons, and other supplies that may have been available.

Flintlock muskets remained the principal arm. Accidents involving weapons continued with the outbreak of war, such as in the case of Stonington militiaman John Miner who was injured by a premature cannon discharge during the defense of his town in 1814. In its rapid-fire haste, the gun crew had likely failed to adequately swab the gun after firing, leaving unextinguished sparks to ignite the next charge of powder as it was being loaded.

During the war, only one militia unit was dispatched for service outside of the state, and it was soon recalled by the governor. Although more than 10,000 men did serve in the state's militia from 1812 to 1815, relatively few experienced combat. The notable exceptions were those who participated in the Battle of Stonington, in a skirmish following the burning of the vessels at Pettipauge, and in several lesser exchanges of fire.

The militia did serve for extended periods on active duty at a number of forts and defensive positions in the state. Locations included Bridgeport, New Haven, Killingworth, Saybrook, Waterford, New London, Groton, Mystic, and Stonington. During their 30- or 60-day deployments, they stood guard at harbors, mouths of rivers, and other key positions. While on active duty, privates received $10.00 per month and sergeants earned $12.00. In contrast, captains received $40.00 per month.[8]

The British threat was very real to these men and to all of Connecticut's citizens, who were well aware of British naval and military power. They also remembered, especially in southeastern Connecticut, that the British had massacred 80 militia defenders of Fort Griswold in Groton following their surrender 30 years earlier during the Revolutionary War.

Some of Connecticut's militia members actually served on the water as a means of assisting with coastal defense. In May of 1814, the General Assembly authorized the deployment of "row-guards … in such harbors of this state as the protection of the state may require & to employ such part of the military force, mariners and boats as may be necessary."[9] In this capacity, the row-guards patrolled harbors at places such as New Haven, watching for threatening British activity. Connecticut troops avoided additional "naval" service during a heightened British threat in August of 1814, when state leaders refused a request by the U.S. Navy to place militia detachments onboard Commodore Decatur's ships at Gales Ferry for added protection.[10]

Life while on active duty could be

challenging—even during times of limited threats from the British. On several different occasions, petitions were filed with the General Assembly by the forces in the vicinity of New London. They protested the poor quality of the rations, muskets, and tents in use by the militia.[11] In the summer of 1813 complaints also arose concerning one of the most valued ration commodities—liquor. A contractor provided cider brandy, which seems to have been closer to vinegar. One officer observed, "a more pernicious poison was never distilled."[12]

Militia duties and responsibilities were generally taken very seriously, especially by officers. Discipline for dereliction of duty could be severe. Private Garritt Osborne of the 37th Regiment of Infantry was found guilty of desertion from his post at Fort Trumbull in July of 1814. His punishment included two months of hard labor with a ball and chain attached to his ankle, stoppage of his liquor ration, shaving smooth of one side of his head twice during his sentence, and placing him on a wooden horse three days each week for two hours each day.[13]

Although actual combat experiences were limited for the militia, they were a reality for men such as Stonington defender Jesse Dean. He recalled in later years that his friends barely recognized him after the battle. He had lost his hat, his hair was knotted, his face was "smutted with smoke" and his clothing was spattered with the blood of his wounded compatriot, John Miner.[14]

Connecticut militia units saw only limited action, yet throughout the war thousands of men stood ready—armed, trained, and willing to defend their state in the face of a serious British threat. When the war ended, the men who were on active duty were quickly released and returned to their homes. The governor of the state praised the militia for "their uniformly spirited and honourable conduct."[15] Today, the tradition continues in the state with the service of modern militiamen—the Connecticut National Guard. But, unlike their forebears of 1812, these defenders of the Nutmeg State have served with honor in the distant and dangerous conflicts in Iran and Afghanistan.

Waterford, the *Ramillies* and a frigate "way anker stand for N.L. at 11oclock being 6 miles south commenc'd a tremendous firing both ships was enveloped for 15 minets the Smoke assended 3 or 4 hundred feet & then anc'r'd near N.L." That threatening exercise coincided with confusion ashore, when General Henry Burbeck received orders from the Secretary of War to dismiss the militia protecting the port. Consequently, all of the state troops were called down from Fort Griswold, mustered at the foot of State Street, addressed by their commander, General Jirah Isham, and dismissed. Between the cannonading and the militia pouring out of the town, panic gripped the populace. A contingent of regular army artillerymen still manned the guns at Fort Trumbull, but not until a week later, when militiamen from Saybrook and Marlborough arrived for duty, did life return to edgy normality.[13]

The British squadron remained especially active that summer and fall as it established control over Long Island Sound. Two weeks of entries from the journal kept by Sylvanus Griswold suggests the level of activity:

[July] 22   1 friget sail'd west anc'r'd of[f] Rocky neck 7p.m. sail'd east to her station
23   1 frigat cruised of[f] Champlins [near New London Light] then over to Gull's Island
24   [The British] took 1 vessel sent to B[lock] island
25   1 vessels Gits [gets] safe to N.L. today
26   the enemy fire a number of cannon
27   Keep their stations fire cannon foggy
28   they fire smartly today
             1 vessel Gits by today
             6 vessels are taken today
             today a . . . schooner from N.L. was chased ashore at Saybrook pint [Point]
             did not take her
29   set fire to a vessel of[f] Saybrook then leave her, our men went on board
             and saved the hul[l]
31   a sloop & a Vinyard [Martha's Vineyard] boat gits by today
             a sloop taken in Plumb Gut (between Orient Point L.I and Plum Island) they
             took out what they pleased & ransom'd for 300$
Aug. 1   2 small vessels sail'd of[f] east today 1 of them sail'd 15 miles west
             today some of our small craft git by today. The Brittions brig git home
3.   friget sail'd west today & back at Knight the Ships now 14 miles south of Champlins

Then, on Sunday, November 28, 1813, a significant action took place between the Royal Navy vessels and approximately 200 local defenders. The incident was triggered when the coasting sloop *Roxana*, bound from New York to Providence, was run ashore about a half mile west of New London Light to escape three barges that were in hot pursuit. The alarm was sounded immediately as the crew rowed ashore, and local residents grabbed their arms and rushed to defend the vessel. The *Gazette* reported that, "a few inhabitants immediately assembled and from an adjacent wall so annoyed the marauders that they abandoned the vessel as soon as they could put fire to her." According to the journal of Sylvanus Griswold, 10 men left the church service in New London, ran to Fort Trumbull, and "took 2 smart field pieces & hastened to the scene of Action & drove the three barges off." A half-hour of steady firing from both sides ensued as American reinforcements arrived. Some of the locals boarded the vessel to try and retrieve what they could, but were driven off when the frigate *Statira* approached and fired two or three broadsides at the burning vessel. The affair carried on for much of the day, and local commanders General Burbeck, Commodore Decatur, and Captain Jones came to observe. It was estimated that, between the frigate *Statiria* and the sloop of war *Loup Cervier*, 20 broadsides were fired at the defenders on the beach, who were fully exposed to the fire but miraculously sustained no casualties. The *Gazette* mocked that, "the plowing Stackpoole [Captain Hassard Stackpoole of HMS *Statira*] gave to Rogers's land is a fair offset to the holes he made in his barn, crib and back-house."[14]

As the next chapter makes clear, local residents found many ways to resist the power of the Royal Navy. Nevertheless, the British blockading squadron largely accomplished its mission in keeping Decatur's squadron bottled up and choking off the coastal trade routes. In time, the flow of commercial traffic on Long Island Sound, both east and west, was reduced to a bare trickle.[15]

CHAPTER THREE

The Battle of Long Island Sound[1]

THE SHELTERED WATERS OF LONG ISLAND SOUND were the scene of a number of fierce and unlikely encounters in the War of 1812, some of them featuring surprisingly advanced weaponry not usually associated with the age of fighting sail, including rockets, submarines, and torpedoes. Lurking just off stage was a heavily armored catamaran, the world's first steam-powered warship, that never quite made it into battle but which would have created a sensation had she been launched in time. The Battle of Long Island Sound, which flared up sporadically throughout 1813 and 1814, represents an early example of a very modern military concept known as asymmetric warfare, in which a large, expensive military organization (the Royal Navy) must contend with a small, loosely organized enemy (the population living along the shore of the Sound), and where neither side can be said to hold the upper hand. In this respect it resembles the wars the United States has fought in Asia and the Middle East over the past half century.

Principle figures in this anachronistic conflict include the American inventor and entrepreneur Robert Fulton who provided much of the lethal hardware, along with Commodore Stephen Decatur, America's most celebrated naval hero. The British side was commanded by the equally celebrated Commodore Sir Thomas Masterman Hardy, who had been Nelson's flag captain at Trafalgar. Most of the other important warriors were civilian adventurers waging war as much for profit as for patriotism.

Fulton's involvement began in Europe, years before the war, when he tried to interest first France and then Britain in what he always considered his most important invention, his underwater bombs which he called "torpedoes." These were not like the modern self-propelled explosives we are familiar with, but something closer to what we call sea mines. Like modern torpedoes they were powerful enough to sink large ships. When neither Napoleon nor the Royal Navy showed sufficient interest in his torpedoes, Fulton returned to America, and after pausing long enough to design and build the world's first practical steamboat, the *Clermont* (1807), he wrote and published a book called *Torpedo War and Submarine Explosions* (1810) as a means of getting the US government interested in his torpedoes. The book explained the various different ways his torpedoes could sink ships, and showed how, under the right conditions, even a single individual in a rowboat had the ability to destroy a large ship-of-the-line with a crew of 500 or more.

After war with Britain was declared in June 1812, Fulton lobbied Congress on behalf of his torpedoes, and he encouraged passage of the Torpedo Act in March 1813, a bill specifically designed to make life difficult for the Royal Navy:

> AN ACT TO ENCOURAGE THE DESTRUCTION
> OF THE ARMED VESSELS OF WAR OF THE ENEMY
>
> Be it enacted by the Senate and House of Representatives of the United States of America in Congress assembled—That during the present war with Great Britain it shall be lawful for any person or persons to burn, sink or destroy any British armed vessels… and for that purpose to use torpedoes, submarine instruments, or any other destructive machines whatever, And a bounty of one half the value of the armed vessels so burnt, sunk or destroyed, and also one-half of the value of her guns, cargo, tackle and apparel shall be paid out of the treasury of the United States to such person or persons who shall effect the same otherwise than by the armed or commissioned vessels of the United States.

In short, Congress was encouraging a whole new category of warfare. By offering prize money to anyone with a rowboat and an explosive device Congress opened the door for a remarkable series of mischief-makers.

Three months after Congress passed the Torpedo Act, the war came to Long Island Sound when Commodore Stephen Decatur, in command of a little squadron of three warships, stole out of New York and attempted to slip past the blockade, only to be spotted by HMS *Ramillies* and *Orpheus* off Montauk Point. The Royal Navy promptly gave chase, and to avoid capture, Decatur was forced to retreat to the safety of New London Harbor. The British immediately took up permanent station outside. The frustrated Decatur, with his three warships—the 44-gun *United States*, the 38-gun *Macedonian*, and the 18-gun *Hornet*—was determined to get his three ships out to sea, but the much larger British naval force under Commodore Hardy was equally determined to keep him right where he was.

On June 15, 1813, just two weeks after Decatur's narrow escape into New London, an enterprising businessman in New York named John Scudder Jr. put the finishing touches to a complicated machine of destruction designed to make him and his partners a lot of money. It was a schooner they had recently purchased and totally refurbished named the *Eagle*. In the hold they had planted a large cask filled with ten 40-pound kegs of gunpowder, with a quantity of sulphur mixed into it. They surrounded the cask with huge stones, so placed that in the event of an explosion they would be hurled outward under tremendous force and, it was hoped, inflict great damage and injury. Scudder then fixed two flintlocks to this lethal contraption, cocked to strike the sparks that would ignite the gunpowder. Cords of twine led from the flintlocks to two innocent looking barrels of flour in the hatch, and the cords were attached in such a way that moving the barrels would set off the flintlocks and ignite the enormous booby trap down below. A prodigious explosion would result. The

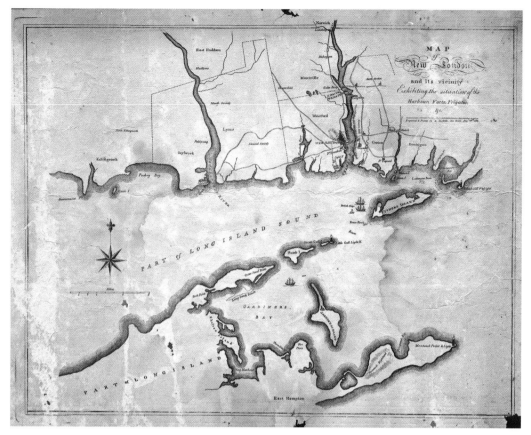

Amos Doolittle of New Haven produced this engraved map in 1813. Among its details are the positions of the American naval ships in the Thames River near Gales Ferry and the British blockading squadron in their usual position off Fishers Island and in Gardiner's Bay. Although the British did initiate several damaging attacks—most notably at Essex (Pettipauge), Stonington, and Killingworth — the ongoing disruption of American shipping proved to be the most potent effect of the blockade.

(New London County Historical Society, 1909.02)

entire *Eagle,* from stem to stern was in fact a single self-propelled floating bomb and a very expensive one at that; but as far as Scudder and his partners were concerned she was an excellent investment. They had rigged her for the sole purpose of sinking Commodore Hardy's flagship, the 74-gun *Ramillies,* and if the bomb proved successful, the investors stood to receive 150 thousand dollars in prize money, the equivalent of millions in today's currency.

Under the command of a Captain Riker, the *Eagle* sailed down the Sound, and anchored off Millstone Point about eleven o'clock on the morning of June 25, 1813. Captain Riker deliberately placed her within tempting distance of the enemy, then rowed ashore with his crew. Soon, a barge crewed by an officer and 20 sailors set out from the *Ramillies* to capture the schooner.

As soon as the British reached the *Eagle,* Riker and his crew, safely hidden in the shrubbery, began such an intense and accurate musket fire that the British had to cut the anchor cable to move her out of range quickly. The unsuspecting British then sailed her back under the guns of the blockading squadron. The *Eagle* appeared to be a valuable prize, heavily laden with marine stores and provisions. But because she now had no anchor the British had to tie her alongside another vessel in order to make an inspection of her cargo, as her owners had planned. The obvious vessel to secure her to was the flagship, and British tars worked for nearly two hours to get her alongside the *Ramillies.* As luck would have it the wind died away and the tide worked against their efforts to secure the *Eagle.* Commodore Hardy, who had been watching his men's futile efforts, finally ordered them to move the *Eagle* away from the *Ramillies* and tie her to a sloop captured several days earlier and now anchored

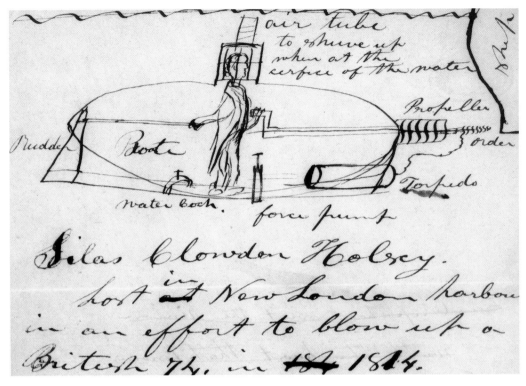

about three-quarters of a mile away. Almost assuredly, his decision saved his flagship.

At half past two that afternoon someone on board the *Eagle* hoisted one of the flour barrels, triggering the flintlocks, and the terrible engine of death erupted. Captain Riker, still watching from Millstone Point, reported later, "The body of fire appeared to rise upwards of 900 feet into the air, with a black streak on the spout side, and then burst like a rocket." The explosion was so great that a shower of pitch and tar fell on the deck of the *Ramillies*, almost a mile away. A Royal Navy lieutenant and 10 sailors simply disappeared in the explosion, along with the *Eagle* and the schooner to which she was moored.

The effect of the *Eagle* incident on Captain Hardy is difficult to overstate. The enormity of the attack—the deceit, the trickery, the underhanded manner of the operation—the fact that the *Ramillies* owed her survival to good luck alone—these facts must have deeply shaken Hardy. This "new mode of warfare," as he characterized it, was antithetical to everything in which he believed, "he never having used even hand grenades in any vessel he has commanded." The idea of "civilized war" was thrown into a cocked hat, and to someone of Hardy's stripe, the *Eagle* incident must have seemed like the opening of the gates of Chaos itself. He ordered a new and more rigorous patrol of Long Island Sound calculated to neutralize these troubled waters, and dispatched an angry note to the American militia leader at New London, General Jirah Isham: "I am under the necessity of requesting you to make it publicly known that I cannot permit vessels or boats of any description (flags of truce excepted) to approach or pass the British squadron, in consequence of an American vessel having exploded yesterday, three hours after she was in our possession."[2]

But the attacks continued. There was simply too much money to be made, and too many ambitious Yankees eager to make it. Just two weeks after the *Eagle* explosion a shadowy figure, described by the *New York Herald* only as a mysterious and unnamed "gentleman from Norwich," introduced another new element into the War of 1812: submarines. In fact there was nothing all that mysterious about the gentleman. He was 26-year-old Silas Plowden Halsey of Preston, Connecticut, and according to a July 10, 1813, story in the *Herald*, he had developed a "diving boat" and had managed on three occasions to submerge his craft off New London and maneuver it under the *Ramillies*, with the intent of blowing a hole in her bottom. On his first attempt, after remaining underwater for a considerable length of time, he ran short of air and had to surface only a few feet from the target ship, where a sentinel immediately spotted him and gave the alarm. According to the *Herald,* Halsey hastily submerged again to avoid the musket fire directed at him. The *Ramillies* cut her cables and got under way with all possible dispatch. On a subsequent night Halsey again tried to get underneath the *Ramillies*, this time without success. On his third attempt he came up directly under his target and fastened his boat to her keel, where he remained for half an hour, eventually succeeding in drilling a hole through her copper sheathing. He then tried to attach a watertight bomb to the drill lodged solidly in her bottom. The apparatus included a clockwork device as a detonator. Unfortunately for Halsey, the auger broke and he was left with nothing to attach the bomb to. He had to abandon the attempt. Sometime afterward, he was lost when his submarine sank.[3]

The story of a "Bushnell II" submarine, coming so close on the heels of the *Eagle* incident, clearly signaled that the United States in general, and a group of its citizens living principally along the boundaries of Long Island Sound in particular, was moving towards a radically new understanding of the nature of naval warfare. Certainly Hardy must have come to that conclusion. He announced his intention to retain on board of his blockading vessels every prisoner taken from New London, in the hope that their presence might discourage local torpedoists from attacking his ships. In addition, he gave orders to all squadron vessels to avoid remaining anchored in a single place for any longer than was absolutely necessary," and he caused the bottom of the *Ramillies* to be swept by a cable every two hours, night and day, to protect her from what he called "those damned Yankee barnacles."[4]

Meanwhile, Commodore Decatur, champing at the bit to escape into the Atlantic. The *Ramillies* and *Orpheus* were anchored in Gardiner's Bay (safe from submarines and torpedoes), and Decatur had learned that Hardy regularly took lunch on Gardiner's Island. At the end of July he hatched a plan to kidnap the British commander while he was at table. Today it sounds like a harebrained scheme—it *was* a harebrained scheme—but Decatur was desperate and had little choice. Hardy was a national hero back in England, and Decatur calculated that he might be able to bargain freedom for his squadron in exchange for the return of such a distinguished officer.

Four boats set out on the windy night of July 26, led by a local Long Island mariner from Oysterponds named Joshua Penny. Midshipman Abraham Ten Eyck's boat landed on Gardiner's Island in the morning. When a British boat arrived, the Americans seized the occupants, but the highest ranking officer was a lieutenant, not Captain Hardy. Realizing they had been seen from the *Ramillies*, they parolled their nine captives and escaped to Long Island, returning to New London the following night, emptyhanded.[5]

Still searching for a way to punch his way free of the blockade, Decatur consulted with his friend Robert Fulton, who had come up with a remarkable idea—a huge steam powered catamaran with her engine and paddlewheel protected between the two hulls, and armed with twenty-four 32-pounders. Fulton planned to call her *Demologos*, literally "the voice of the people." Such a ship, without mast or sails, could lurk safely in harbor until the wind died down, then with the blockading fleet immobilized and swinging helplessly at anchor, she would fire up her engine and steam out at a stately

The Blue Lights

written by Andrew W. German

COMMODORE DECATUR brought his squadron partway down the river at the end of October, but the *United States* grounded and damaged her rudder, so his escape plans were delayed. Hearing that an admiral and two fireships were expected to join the British squadron, Decatur anchored his squadron off New London's Market Wharf on December 3, with the British squadron anchored six miles south. On the blustery night of Sunday, December 12, he planned to slip out of the harbor and run past the anchored British ships to the open sea. But rumors of his departure had spread, and unidentified parties schemed to warn the British squadron. As the ships prepared to raise their anchors and run, lookouts on the *Hornet* and the boat guard of the *Macedonian* noticed blue lights shining on Groton Heights and down toward New London Light. Looking to sea, they saw signal lights on one of the British ships. Fearing the British were ready for him, Decatur postponed his squadron's departure.[1]

Although many questioned the blue lights, suggesting they were signal lights on patrolling barges rather than signals communicated from shore, Decatur stood by the report of his officers and men. With its loyalty impugned, the community had an uncomfortable feeling that there were "traitorous wretches" among them. "While we ever will be proud of maintaining the patriotism of our own state, yet we are not so far converts to the *French* doctrine of 'the perfectibility of human nature,' as to assert that Connecticut is pure, and therefore that no foreign spy or domestic traitor can be harbored in her bosom," wrote Samuel Green of the *Connecticut Gazette.*[2]

When blue lights blazed again at 10:00 p.m. on Sunday, January 9, and militia and naval officers saw them answered by all the British ships, it was clear that the British had agents ashore, who would warn them if Decatur made a move. He moved his vessels back up the Thames on January 27.[3]

Some continued to maintain that the lights were only imagined by jumpy officers. Others have imagined that Elizabeth Stewart, wife of the former British counsel James Stewart, coordinated the signaling, but Decatur did not express suspicion of the Stewarts. Connecticut Marshal Robert Fairchild suspected the surveyor of the port and another "patriotic" resident, who had ingratiated themselves with Decatur, of being secret agents for the British. A Captain Center of Newport was detained for questioning, and an unfounded rumor of the seizure of a female spy circulated through town. The *Connecticut Gazette* lamented those "who are so polluted by the love of money, and so dead to every patriotic feeling, as to be in the habit of furnishing the enemy with beef, poultry, butter, &c.," implying there were many possible suspects who consorted with the British. To spread the blame the paper remarked, "boats have been seen to pass from the Connecticut river, not circuitously, but in a direct course to the enemy's ships lying off this harbor."[4]

In retrospect, Dr. Samuel H.P. Lee of New London remarked that blue lights were often seen along shore during the blockade, and in the dark it was very difficult to determine if they emanated from land or sea. He also claimed that, in his experience, British officers

With a population of 261,942 in 1810, Connecticut had 20 percent of New England's people and strongly supported New England's largely Federalist politics. Along with six other states, Connecticut voted for the Federalist presidential candidate, DeWitt Clinton of New York, in 1812, but ten states (and half of Maryland) supported Republican President James Madison for a second term and continuation of the war. Amos Doolittle engraved this map about 1800.

(© Mystic Seaport, Maps and Charts Collection, Mystic, CT)

and seamen in disguise often lurked in New London and traveled through Connecticut and even to New York, acting as secret agents for the blockaders. Lee believed the British were so well informed of Decatur's moves that blue-light signals were unnecessary. Looking back on the war, and offended by the accusations of Federalist disloyalty, Lee and ex-militiaman Samuel Goodrich dismissed Decatur's blue-lights claim.[5]

The blue lights brought to light the hidden divisions of loyalty, Yankee opportunism, and principled opposition to the war that characterized New London and Connecticut. And more broadly, the blue lights became a semantic symbol of disloyalty, "blue-light Federalist" becoming the ultimate insult during the last year of the war.[6]

four miles an hour to meet the hapless foe. With absolute control of his own movements, the captain could reach a safe position where the enemy could not return fire, and at his leisure supervise the complete destruction of the blockading squadron with broadside after uninterrupted broadside. Decatur, Jones, and Biddle all endorsed Fulton's proposal for the ship at New London on January 9, 1814.[6]

It was a magnificent idea, but at best it would take many months to build such a vessel, and Decatur did not have the time. Instead he came up with another desperate scheme. By flag of truce he sent a letter to Hardy proposing that the frigates under their command fight a duel. It was a curious suggestion, and it was only with regret that Hardy turned it down.

Towards the end of winter, the torpedoes returned to Long Island Sound. One night in March, 1814, merchant captain Jeremiah Holmes of Mystic set out with a crew in his 16-oar galley *Young Hornet* to attack the frigate *Endymion*, anchored near the Dumplings off the west end of Fishers Island. He and his crew were carrying a very different kind of torpedo than the compact designs of Robert Fulton. Designed by Mr. Riker of the *Eagle* plot, it consisted principally of a 30-foot hollow cylinder fashioned of tin plate, about seven inches in diameter. It contained 75 pounds of superfine gunpowder, and was designed to float on buoys. Near one end was a crossbar about 12 feet in length with hooks at either end that perforated the cylinder.

The plan was to position the boat up-tide of the *Endymion* and let the torpedo out on a line in such a way that the tide carried it to the target. Once there, it was hoped, the hooks on the crossbar would catch on some line or protrusion, and the force of the tide on the cylinder would eventually turn the torpedo at an oblique angle to the crossbar, tripping a spring and causing the bomb to explode.

From the beginning the attack did not go well. By the time they were paying out the torpedo from the boat, the tide had turned to flood. Then they realized that the line attached to the floating bomb was too stiff to work freely, and it fouled on something hidden on the sea bottom. When they tried to free it, they succeeded only in pulling the torpedo underwater, where it too got caught. The men worked frantically throughout most of the night to free the torpedo; but after several hours of fruitless effort they finally gave up, cut the line, and abandoned the weapon, rowing disconsolately back to shore.

Less than two weeks later, on March 24, Holmes was back with a second torpedo. This time his target was a 74-gun ship-of-the-line. The Americans thought she was the *Ramillies*, but in fact Hardy had been temporarily called away, and the blockade was now under the command of Captain Thomas Capel of HMS *La Hogue*. Holmes had coordinated with Decatur on his plan, so the American warships in the Thames River were all on alert, hoping that the attack on the blockading ship would create enough confusion to allow them to escape.

Guided only by faint moonlight, Jeremiah Holmes slipped past Eastern Point and around the dark shape of the *La Hogue*, coming up to the northwest of her and dropping anchor. This time the men caught the tide, and the rope was properly flexible. After paying out the torpedo for a considerable distance, and feeling the gratifying pull of the tide directing it toward the target ship, Holmes ordered the anchor raised. The oarsmen tried to row eastward toward the land, so as to swing the torpedo against the ship, but the fresh northwest wind and strong ebb tide carried the boat down so near the bow of the *La Hogue* that they could clearly make out the sails furled on her jibboom.

Realizing their danger, they hauled the boat up to windward and anchored, all the time trying to haul in on the torpedo. They managed to pull the bomb up near the *La Hogue*'s bow, but the hauling line caught in the anchor cable. A sudden strain on the crossbar tripped the detonator, and the torpedo exploded at exactly 2:45 in the morning, shattering the night's silence and sending a huge column of

The YANKEY TORPEDO.

water into the air, soaking a half dozen terrified sailors on the *La Hogue*.

Instantly, a storm of musketry poured down from the ship's deck, without effect. Holmes pulled desperately for shore as the *La Hogue* fired her cannons and set signals for the other blockading vessels. Decatur, waiting to hear that the 74 was disabled and at least temporarily out of action, heard an excited version of the failed attack and realized he had run out of luck and lost his last chance to escape. The British would now be so thoroughly alarmed and on their guard against such attacks that there was no possibility of another attempt. Three weeks later he had his ships moved farther upriver and ordered the *United States* and *Macedonian* to be dismantled.[7]

A direct offshoot of Jeremiah Holmes's attack on the *La Hogue* was the highly successful British attack on the shipping at Pettipaugue on the Connecticut River.

Early in the summer of 1814, a new kind of vessel found her way into Long Island Sound, a torpedo boat created in New York by a Mr. Berrien, and built specifically to operate against the blockading fleet off New London. Berrien had christened her the *Turtle*, in honor of Bushnell's original, but unlike that one-man submersible the new *Turtle* was operated by a crew of 12 and was only a semisubmersible, incapable of diving. It was in all likelihood propelled by a hand-cranked paddlewheel.

On June 26, 1814 the *Turtle* was heading towards Gardiner's Bay to attack the blockading fleet when she was washed ashore by a gale at Horton's Point near Southold, Long Island. One member of the crew who attempted to swim to shore during the storm drowned, but the others survived by staying with the vessel until it grounded. By that time the British had spotted the *Turtle*, and barges from the frigate *Maidstone* and sloop-of-war *Sylph* were sent in to destroy it. With the help of local

The Burning of the Fleet
The British Raid on Essex, April 7-8, 1814
written by Jerry Roberts

ON APRIL 8, 1814, the United States suffered its greatest single maritime loss of the war. According to the official British report to the Admiralty, 27 American vessels, including several privateers, were burned at Pettipauge on the Connecticut River. The devastating raid was chronicled in newspapers across the nation, yet today the event is virtually forgotten outside the picturesque village, which was renamed Essex a few years after the raid. Each spring a dozen fife-and-drum corps led by Essex's own Sailing Masters of 1812 parade down Main Street, marking the worst day in the town's 300-year history.

Some call it the Loser's Day Parade, others call it Burning of the Fleet Day, but many townspeople and tourists alike aren't quite sure what to make of this quintessentially quirky New England tradition. The folklore that has grown up around this event includes burning ships, a boy hero, a well-paid local traitor, mysterious Free Mason connections, and stolen rum. Leaving the legends aside, the facts themselves are pretty amazing, as on April 7, 1814, the British came to burn the privateers of Pettipauge.

Settled in 1648, Pettipauge became a colonial port trading with the West Indies and ports along the Eastern Seaboard. By the early 1700s it had become a significant shipbuilding center in support of growing maritime commerce. During the American Revolution, the Connecticut frigate *Oliver Cromwell* had been built there, and the world's first operational combat submarine, the *Turtle*, was constructed nearby. By the beginning of the

nineteenth century, Pettipauge had evolved into a bustling river port and seafaring community with shipyards, chandleries, blacksmith shops, warehouses, and a 900-foot-long ropewalk.[1]

During the War of 1812, the British blockade of Long Island Sound strangled shipping along the Connecticut coast. With merchant vessels sitting idle, some owners began to convert them to privateers, and in towns like Pettipauge vessels were being built specifically for that task.

To avoid the tedious work of hunting these vessels down at sea one by one, the Royal Navy elected to destroy them at their source whenever possible. Pettipauge was a known location where privateers were being fitted out. A newspaper ad in New York even solicited investment in one of the new privateers being built here. The challenge for the British was that Pettipauge lay six miles up the Connecticut River, and the massive sand bars at its mouth prevented large naval ships from going upriver. To meet this challenge, Richard Coote, captain of HMS *Borer*, was put in command of a special raiding force consisting of 136 Royal Marines and seamen drawn from the crews of four warships in the blockading squadron. On the night of April 7, 1814, they embarked in six heavily armed rowboats and headed up stream.[2]

The British first attacked the fort at Old Saybrook in order to avoid being trapped on the way out, but two years into the war they found it empty, unmanned, and without guns. They proceeded upriver and arrived at Pettipauge at 3:30 on the morning of the 8th. According to Captain Coote's report to the Admiralty, "on approaching it we found the town alarmed, the Militia all on the alert, and apparently disposed with the assistance of one 4 lb. Gun to oppose our landing, however after the discharge of the Boats' Guns and a volley of Musketry from our Marines, they prudently ceased firing and gave us no further interruption."[3]

From the perspective of the volunteer militiamen on the beach, the heavy barrage from the river must have been overwhelming. No one had expected this sort of thing so far inland. Over the years since the battle, cannon balls and musket shot have been found lodged in houses and hillsides along Main Street, some nearly a quarter mile from the landing site.

The Royal Marines swiftly secured the village against counterattack and proceeded up Main Street at least as far as Bushnell's Tavern, now the Griswold Inn. Here, Lieutenant Lloyd, in command of the Marines, is said to have read a proclamation from Captain Coote announcing it was only their intent to destroy shipping; that no harm would befall the local residents, unless they resisted. In that case, he announced, the torch would be put to the entire town.[4]

Met with the overwhelming force already in the village, the citizens had little choice but to stand in the shadows as the British did their work. The best they could do was to send riders off into the night to alert local militia and government forces in New London.

While the marines held the town, the seamen set about burning all of the vessels that lay at anchor in the river, alongside the wharves, and under construction on the stocks. True to their word, the British set no major waterfront buildings afire. They warped vessels away from the wharves before setting them ablaze, and they made a meticulous record of the name, tonnage, and rig of each vessel they torched. In one of the folk legends of the raid, local teenager Austin Lay is said to have repeatedly attempted to douse fires aboard one of the burning ships despite the presence of so many British sailors.

His story was chronicled in the children's book, *The Sea Lady*. Meanwhile, other British sailors destroyed or commandeered canvas and cordage from the waterfront warehouses as well as a substantial quantity of rum, a valued commodity in the days when every American and British soldier and sailor was issued half a pint a day.

With the light of dawn, the British located other vessels in North Cove and sent boat crews to burn them as well. By 10:00 a.m. they had put the torch to six ships, four brigs, six schooners, nine sloops, and several smaller craft, but it was broad daylight and they were six miles deep in American territory.[5] Captain Coote knew it was time to leave.

The British began an orderly departure with their ships' boats and two captured privateers, the brig *Young Anaconda* and the schooner *Eagle*, filled with the rum, sails, and cordage. Meanwhile, Killingworth militiamen under Lieutenant Bray were approaching the west bank of the river with their cannon, and after the express rider reached New London about 12:30 p.m., government forces were dispatched toward the east bank of the river. Captain French's militia artillery set off with a fieldpiece, and some U.S. Marines from Commodore Decatur's squadron and some civilian volunteers left in carriages. Marines and a company of infantry from Fort Trumbull followed on foot.[6]

On the way downstream, the captured brig went aground on one of the river's shifting sand bars. While being subject to ineffectual gunfire from shore, the British transferred everything from the grounded vessel and then burned it. A little further downriver, Coote anchored his boats and captured schooner and decided to stay put until nightfall to avoid passing through the narrower parts of the river in broad daylight. That afternoon the British were served with a surrender ultimatum from the growing American forces. Coote simply dismissed it, reporting, "tho sensible of their humane intentions, we set their power to detain us at defiance."[7]

In reality, however, the race was on. Hundreds of American militiamen from nearby towns, and the fieldpiece and carriages full of Marines from New London, had reached the riverbanks by 4:00 p.m. to prevent the British escape. At 7:00 p.m., the British set fire to the remaining privateer and headed downstream in the six ships' boats.[8]

An eyewitness to all of this was American Captain Jeremiah Glover, who claimed to have been captured by the British while trying to save his vessel as it burned in the harbor. After the raid he was released on Fishers Island and wrote an affidavit defending himself against accusations that he piloted the British down the river. Whatever the case, British documents confirm that $2,000 dollars was paid to an American who guided the British during the raid. No name was attached to this record.[9]

The British boats drifted quietly downstream until, off Old Lyme, they were illuminated by bonfires on the shore. Picket boats in the river carried torches to reveal the escaping enemy. As they ran the gauntlet, the British were subject to intense cannon and musket fire from both sides of the river. Coote reported, "I believe no Boat escaped without receiving more or less shot." Despite the effort to stop them, however, by 10:00 p.m. the British boats reached their warships anchored off Saybrook. Coote's party had lost only two marines killed and two sailors injured.[10]

As the *Connecticut Gazette* concluded: "Thus ended an expedition achieved with the smallest loss to the enemy, and the greatest in magnitude of damage that has occurred on the seaboard since the commencement of the War." According to the Captain Coote's official report to the Admiralty, the British set fire to 27 vessels totaling 5,000 tons, including at least six vessels they believed were privateers capable of mounting 130 guns. Although several of the vessels were saved or salvaged, the raid still represents the largest single attack on American shipping during the war. The maritime loss to Essex was staggering. [11]

A permanent exhibit at the Connecticut River Museum, located on the landing site, features a dramatic 16-foot-long mural of the landing, along with such artifacts of the raid as weapons, cannon balls, and burned timbers from some of the ships. It is an event that still lingers in the consciousness of this now peaceful New England village. Main Street is still lined with more than 24 houses that were there when the British came ashore nearly 200 years ago. Today, at the historic Griswold Inn, many a glass is still raised in remembrance of the night when the British brought the War of 1812 to town, stole good Yankee rum, and burned the privateers of Pettipauge.

farmers and militia, the *Turtle*'s crew frantically tried to dismantle the craft to protect whatever secrets she contained. They managed to remove the spiral wheel by which the boat moved, as well as the rudder and crank and any torpedoes she may have been carrying, but when the British marines came on shore the Americans were forced to retreat.

The British had been acutely aware of the *Turtle* for some time and had kept a close eye on her construction in New York. They were convinced she was the brainchild of Robert Fulton, and described her as such. More likely, while the torpedoes she carried might have been Fulton's, the boat itself was another man's design. At the time Berrien was busy constructing the *Turtle*, Fulton had more than enough to handle developing not only his steam powered catamaran, but another submarine as well.

Several British officers made their way to the strange craft and examined it warily, cautiously checking for any live explosive charges. Then they began carefully sketching it and measuring its dimensions. She was 23 feet long with a breadth of 10 feet. Her top was arched like a turtle shell and immensely strong. She had the scantlings of a 100-ton ship, which supported wooden top planking eight inches thick that was in turn cased over with half-inch plate iron. Lieutenant Bowen of the *Maidstone* reported that she was "so strongly and well constructed that a shot cannot penetrate, or can anything grapple with it."

Bowen's report stated that the semisubmersible drew six feet of water, leaving only one foot of boat exposed above the surface. This ironclad deck was painted a dirty white to camouflage it. According to the British the *Turtle* was designed to tow five floating torpedoes, each on its own lead. The report was unable to explain how the crew would use those weapons against enemy ships. After gleaning all the information possible from the beached *Turtle*, Lieutenant Bowen ordered an explosive charge placed on board and moments later, with an explosion heard across the Sound in New London, she disappeared into splinters.[8]

The destruction of the semisubmersible on Horton's Beach marks the end of torpedo warfare

This Congreve rocket was fired at Stonington by the British in August 1814. Designed to burn and essentially self-destruct, surviving examples of fired Congreve rockets are extremely rare. Although they created a dramatic and frightening sight, they caused little damage. On August 10, 1814, during the Battle of Stonington, militiaman David Tracey Jr., who was stationed at Fort Trumbull in New London, wrote: "The Congreve rockets, of which they threw a considerable number. . . . rose apparently some hundreds of feet in the air. In fact they must have done so to have been seen so plain at the distance of 14 miles."

(Rocket, courtesy of Stonington Historical Society, 2008.0045; letter, Connecticut Historical Society)

in the War of 1812. Berrien's *Turtle* was the final entrant in the strange, motley parade of gimcrackery and genius, the last of a line of terror-craft created out of a potent but dangerous mixture of Yankee ingenuity and lust for prize money.

But if the civilians who lived along the shores of Long Island Sound had run out of novel new ways to spread death and destruction at sea, the man who controlled the waters of the Sound still had one more trick up his sleeve. Sir Thomas Hardy, who with judicious effort and considerable patience had somehow managed to maintain the blockade for a year and a half with only negligible losses to his forces, chose the second week of August, 1814, to introduce the citizens of Connecticut to one of the most feared new weapons of the day, the Congreve rocket.

Military rockets were still new, but they had already acquired a formidable reputation. The British had first encountered them in India, where in 1799 the army of Tipu Sultan had used his Mysorean rockets with devastating effect against troops of the East India Company in the siege of Seringapatam. The Royal Arsenal began a rocket program in 1801, and the resulting solid-fuel missile was first demonstrated by William Congreve in 1805. The Royal Navy used Congreve rockets to set fire to Boulogne in 1806 and destroy Copenhagen in 1807. In America, Admiral Sir George Cockburn's squadron first used Congreve rockets during the assault on Lewes, Delaware, in April 1813. Hardy would use them against the village of Stonington, Connecticut.[9]

How the villagers dealt with the Royal Navy bombardment is covered in the next chapter.

CHAPTER FOUR

"The Attack Upon Stonington Point in 1814"[1]

BY 1814 LONG ISLAND SOUND suffered under a tight naval blockade that crippled trade and created alarms along the entire Sound. During the War of 1812, Frances Manwaring Caulkins—who turned 17 two months before the war commenced—lived in the home of her maternal uncle, Christopher Manwaring, high on Manwaring Hill in New London. She later wrote, "Seated on a high rock we watched the motions of the British blockading fleet, and I wrote various belligerent verses, which, however, my uncle said were wanting in *fire* and *fury*—they needed a supply of thunder to make them popular, and I consigned them to the flames." Perhaps then, or else in later years, she collected newspaper articles that chronicled the difficulties facing New London men during the blockade.

Frances Manwaring Caulkins (1795-1869) could trace her lineage in New London back to 1651. Frances was educated in Norwich but often spent time at her Uncle Christopher Manwaring's home in New London, from where she saw the British blockaders in 1813-14. After many years of teaching in Norwich and New London, she settled permanently in New London in 1842 and began to write fulltime while engaging in religious and philanthropic work. Her best-known works, *History of Norwich, Connecticut* (1845) and *History of New London, Connecticut* (1852), are thoroughly researched and well written, as is her account of her trip to research the Battle of Stonington. This carte-de-visite photograph was taken about 1861.

(New London County Historical Society, Giles Bishop Album 779 N461 66B)

Caulkins eventually wrote critically acclaimed histories of Norwich and New London, but her unpublished manuscripts provide evidence that, nearly twenty years before she published her first book, she worked on a history of the British attack on Stonington in 1814. She also wrote about the wider conflict of the war and tried to determine why the war occurred. And she transcribed marine notes from various sources, tracing the comings and goings of vessels in New London harbor and up and down eastern Long Island Sound, and documenting the impact of war on the maritime communities.

In 1828, when she was 33 years old and living in Norwich, Caulkins visited the town of Stonington. She wrote a humorous letter about that trip, detailing the hazardous carriage ride though Poquetonnock behind the hard-mouthed steed named General Jackson. Once in Stonington, she stayed at the home of Jesse Dean, one of the surviving defenders of the town, and she wrote that during the first evening, "they had a great historical time." She added, "the most interesting points of history that we discussed were the attacks on the village of Stonington point."

The next day, Jesse Dean drove Caulkins to the Point. In Stonington Caulkins became a serious historian, and Dean was her informant. "With patient kindness, he exhibited and explained everything curious and interesting that came in our way."

"At the Point we visited the spot where stood the battery so famous in the bombardment of the place in August 1814. It was now covered with lumber and all the confused materials of a shipyard." Dean himself had stood next to one of the young defenders when the youth suffered a wound from flying debris and had "supported him in his arms to a place of safety, his garments sprinkled with blood."

From the lighthouse, built in 1823, Dean pointed out to Caulkins "the spot to which one of the cannon was dragged during the attack of 1814, to repel the British when they moved round to the West. This was very near the Lighthouse." Dean also described "the situation of the British fleet during the bombardment, showing me where each vessel lay at the most critical periods of those four days of alarm and danger. We then went to the house where Widow Hall, the sick woman, lay and where she died during the bombardment. This was at the center of ruin, and many houses were much shattered by the bombs and shells of the enemy."

Caulkins's goal for the visit was clear: to learn as much as possible about the British attack. She met with surviving participants and eyewitnesses of the battle, and she toured the battle site itself, viewing the battle souvenirs that many residents still displayed in the yards and on the fence posts. Soon after, she wrote the following history of the battle of Stonington.

NANCY H. STEENBURG

———————————◆◆◆◆◆————————

Stonington Point is a tongue of land about half a mile in length, projecting southerly into Long Island Sound, near its eastern extremity. It is the site of a noted maritime village which was incorporated as a borough in 1801, and at that time distinguished principally for a successful prosecution of the fisheries. It has since engaged with spirit in other paths of commercial enterprise, the coasting and West India trade, sealing, whaling, and ship building.

During the Second War with Great Britain, Long Island Sound was for two years the cruising ground of a British squadron whose principal object was the blockade of New London harbor where two American frigates and a sloop of war had taken refuge. The commander of the blockading squadron was Sir Thomas Masterman Hardy, whose flagship was the *Ramillies*. He had commanded the *Victory* at the battle of Trafalgar and was the personal friend of Lord Nelson whom he supported in his dying moments. Admiral Cochrane was the superior naval officer upon the coast of the United States, the whole fleet being subject to his orders.

The borough of Stonington Point contained at that period about 120 dwellings and shops and between 800 and 900 inhabitants. The only defense of the place consisted of a small semi-circular breastworks or battery, 3 or 4 feet high, thrown up by the citizens, a swivel, or 4-pounder that had been used for festival purposes, and two 18-pounders furnished by the general government and

This Liverpool-style transferware commemorative pitcher was commissioned by Stonington defender Silas Burrows of Mystic about 1820. Although the view condenses four days of battle action into a single moment, it depicts—with some accuracy but a bit of artistic license—the attacking British ships and barges, the Stonington flag, and other elements of the event. In fact, the British ships remained about a mile and a half from Stonington, not as close as they are shown here.

(Courtesy of Stonington Historical Society, 2008.0066)

mounted upon field carriages. At this point a flag-staff was erected and a small guard of militia kept. This was considered a sufficient defense against surprise from any hostile barge or galley that might be prowling on the coast for plunder. No other attack could reasonably be apprehended, for neither honorable renown, nor valuable booty could be gained by the savage [*sic*] of a defenseless, unaggressive village. Therefore, though lying within the view of the blockading squadron, Stonington had not been placed in a state of defense by the government.

On the 9th of August 1814, without any prior alarm, or intimation of impending danger, a detachment from the enemy's squadron was seen approaching the harbor. It consisted of the *Ramillies*

HMS *Terror*

written by Andrew W. German

WHEN HMS *TERROR* joined Captain Sir Thomas Masterman Hardy's squadron about August 8, she brought a new weapon to the War of 1812: the mortar. Designed to fire upward rather than outward, mortars have been used in siege operations on land since the 1400s. The French first took them to sea in the late 1600s against the Barbary States, with two mortars mounted on the deck of a heavily built vessel. The vessel was securely anchored, with springlines on the anchor cables to adjust its angle of aim. These vessels were used against ports or fortifications, raining both terror and destruction from the sky.

The Royal Navy added its first "bomb ship" armed with mortars to the fleet in 1687, and bomb vessels had served as recently as the siege of Copenhagen in 1807. In August 1812, Admiral Sir John Borlase Warren, commander of the North American station, had requested bomb vessels from the Admiralty, "in case it is decided to annoy the coast of America."

Three ship-rigged bomb vessels of the *Vesuvius* class were launched in 1813. One of them, HMS *Terror,* was the fifth bomb vessel of that name built since 1696. Slightly over 100 feet long, she had a deep, full-bodied hull with heavy internal reinforcement to carry the ammunition and provide the buoyancy needed for the seven-ton weight of her 10- and 13-inch mortars. At an angle of 45 degrees, these weapons could drop a shell on a target more than two miles away.

Mortars fired both explosive shells and incendiary carcasses. The 13-inch shells weighed 200 pounds, while the 10-inch shells weighed 70 pounds. Carcasses weighed 150 pounds and had

three 3-inch holes to spread the burning mix of saltpeter, sulfur, tallow, turpentine, and sulfide of antimony within, a highly combustible combination that would flame for about 11 minutes. Royal Navy specifications called for one carcass for every 44 shells.[1]

Commander John Sheridan had just brought the *Terror* across the Atlantic, and as she proceeded up Fishers Island Sound with the frigate *Pactolus* and the brig *Dispatch,* she was readying her mortars for the first use of this weapon "to annoy the coast of America." By the time the action ended, the *Terror* had fired 170 "bombs" at Stonington, according to her sailing master.[2]

HMS *Terror* would leave local waters a week after the battle, bound for the Chesapeake Bay. On September 13-14, she and four other bomb vessels dropped more than 1,500 shells and carcasses on Fort McHenry—"the bombs bursting in air" of Francis Scott Key's *Star Spangled Banner.*

The rugged *Terror* had a second career as an Arctic exploration vessel. Between 1836 and 1845 she participated in one Antarctic and two Arctic expeditions. She was last reported in August 1845, entering Baffin Bay in the far north as part of Sir John Franklin's failed Northwest Passage voyage.

74, the *Pactolus* 38 guns, the *Despatch* [*sic*], a 22-gun brig, and the bombship *Terror*. These vessels were well-known in the Sound, and the whole force was readily ascertained.*

Consternation was suddenly spread through the village. The inhabitants at first knew not whether to flee from their home or to stay by them, but all irresolution was soon dispelled by the receipt of the following communication from Commander Hardy.

"Not wishing to destroy the unoffending inhabitants residing in the town of Stonington, one hour is granted them from the receipt of this to remove out of town."

This note was dated on board the *Pactolus* at half past 5 o'clock P.M.** and No demand was made, no cause was alleged for this unprecedented act of severity. But the officer that bore the flag in answer to their inquiries gave information that Admiral Cochrane had ordered the place to be destroyed, and it would be done effectually. The inhabitants therefore proceeded with all possible dispatch to remove their families. The women and children, laden with a few of their effects, hastily collected, many of them with tears and wailings, left the village and sought temporary shelter in the neighboring groves, barns, and farm houses. It was fortunate that the mildness of the season and the dry state of the atmosphere admitted of encampment in booths, tents, and outhouses without fear of injurious consequences.

The only means of defense lay in the battery. A band of 20 volunteers, each self-impelled, self-commanded, yet moved as by one mind and authority, repaired thither resolved to stand by the guns and at least to keep the enemy from the land. They had hastily collected what powder could be found in the village, but the supply was small. The magistrates dispatched messengers in every direction with information of the expected attack and demands for men and powder. Expresses were also sent to General Cushing, the militia commander of the district and to the Governor of the State, for orders, and thus night set in.

At 8 o'clock the bombardment commenced with a tremendous discharge of Congreve rockets that seemed to inflame the whole atmosphere. The bomb-ship [*Terror*] with several [Congreve rocket-firing] barges and launches stationed at different points, continued till midnight pouring an incessant stream of flaming projectiles upon the town, but with very little effect. It seems incredible that such a number of rockets, carcases [*sic*], and shells, filled with combustibles of highly explosive power and inflammable nature should be sent for such a length of time into a compacted group of more than one hundred wood buildings, yet not one be kindled into flame. Yet such was the fact. Perhaps some buildings took fire and were preserved by daring individuals, but during this first night of the attack there was no organized arrangement made for quenching the fires. This terrific discharge of fireworks during the darkness of the night, accompanied by the rush, the roar, the bursting of such mighty engines, and the clatter they made among the stones and timbers as they fell, was sufficient to dismay the stoutest hearts exposed to its fury.

This mortar shell, fired by HMS *Terror* during the Battle of Stonington, is one of two now flanking the entrance to the grounds of the town's library. It functioned as a bomb. Bombs contained gunpowder and were intended to explode and scatter iron shrapnel. A British officer from the *Terror* claimed they fired 170 mortar rounds while Stonington residents estimated about 300, with a total weight of 50 tons. (Courtesy of Mystic Seaport, Mystic, CT; Photographer: Dennis Murphy)

---

*This squadron had just arrived. HMS *Ramillies* had spent months off New London since the spring of 1813, but was just back from the coast of Maine. The *Pactolus* and *Terror* were new vessels and had just arrived in North American waters, as had the *Dispatch*.

**According to the account of the Stonington magistrates in the *Connecticut Gazette*, September 7, 1814, only the *Pactolus, Terror,* and *Dispatch* came up Fisher's Island Sound the first day, so Hardy was on the *Pactolus* rather than his flagship *Ramillies*.

Throngs of people on the neighboring hills and shores witnessed the mighty pageant, but the volunteers at the battery stood bravely in the midst of it and kept their post during the whole night. Guided in their aim by the light of the rockets and bombs, they answered every blazing discharge with cannon balls to the great annoyance and manifest injury of the enemy. At 12 o'clock the firing ceased and an interval of repose hushed the tumult of the place.

The battery was on the west, or harbor side of the Point, though not far from its extreme end. During the midnight pause the enemy moved their barges to the east side of the Point, in order to avoid the fire from the battery, and at daylight renewed the discharge of bombs and rockets from that quarter. The little band of veterans with an alacrity, bordering on triumph, forthwith proceeded to drag their 4-pounder and one of their larger pieces across the Point. This exploit, with the aid of some militia men of Col. Randall's regiment that had arrived upon the spot, was soon performed. The fire of these pieces soon silenced the enemy on that side and compelled the barges to retreat, one of them being entirely disabled.

[Caulkins included a clipping from the *Connecticut Gazette* of New London, which published the following article on August 10:

> *Several of the enemy's ships came into the Sound on Saturday and Sunday. Their force last evening consisted of seven ships and 2 brigs, having in company 2 sloops supposed to be prizes. Three ships and a brig came to anchor yesterday afternoon (the 9th) in Fishers Island Sound.*
>
> *On Sunday, a flag came up from the frigate* Forth, *Com. Hotham. The object was to obtain permission for James Stewart, Esq. formerly Consul here, to take off his family. Mr. Stewart was on board. General Cushing, we understand, replied that the request would be forwarded to Washington.*
>
> *It is confidently reported that the British fleet have taken formal possession of Montock point and ordered the families who lived there to retire ten miles from the point. Mr. Holt, keeper of the Light House on Gull Island, has been sent off, with his family, and his house was converted into a hospital. The late movements of the enemy have excited apprehensions that some important expedition is in contemplation.*

Caulkins did not mention the breaking news that Mr. Green inserted in that same issue of his weekly paper at the last moment:

The Enemy at Stonington
At 8 o'clock last evening (after this paper was put to press) an express arrived at Gen. Cushing's head-quarters, from Stonington; with information that two frigates and a brig, had arrived in that harbor, and demanded the surrender of the town, or that it should be laid in ashes; to which demand an answer was given that the inhabitants would defend their fire-sides with their lives. At the request of Gen. Cushing, Gen. Williams ordered out the 8th and 30th regiments for the defense of that town. Congreve rockets were fired on shore during the night, without injury; and this morning at sun-rise, a cannonading commenced, and still continues—at 6 o'clock.

The militia have collected in such force as to prevent a landing, but we fear the place will be nearly destroyed, as the enemy are lying within half gun-shot, and our only defence is two long 18 pounders.

The expedition is commanded by Com. Hardy.]

Jeremiah Holmes and the Battle of Stonington

written by Meredith Mason Brown

THE BRITISH NAVAL SQUADRON that bombarded Stonington for four days, in August 1814, overwhelmingly outgunned Stonington's defenders, and yet the British, for all their firepower, did relatively little damage to Stonington before their squadron sailed away. One reason for this surprising outcome is the effect of the small militia battery on the west side of Stonington Point, and particularly the skilled gunnery of Jeremiah Holmes of Mystic.

Holmes's heart was in the fight. He hated the British because they had impressed him into the Royal Navy and kept him there against his will for two and a half years. From mid-1804 to late 1806, and despite his efforts to show that he was an American citizen, and supposedly not subject to impressment, Holmes was forced to serve the British crown. During that impressment, in the midst of the Napoleonic wars, the powerful Royal Navy—the greatest in the world—taught Holmes how to handle naval cannon, loading, aiming, priming, firing, and sponging out the guns. Holmes learned these skills so well he was made captain of a ten-man gun crew in a British man-of-war.[1]

Impressment was an important part of Great Britain's global struggle with the French under Napoleon. Britain's greatest military asset was its navy, but casualties and desertions made it hard to keep its hundreds of ships adequately manned. British law considered anyone who had ever been a British citizen to be subject to impressed service in the Royal Navy, though not people like Holmes who had never been British subjects. However, given its urgent need for manpower and its awareness of the many British subjects sailing on American ships, the Royal Navy tended not to give much credence to the claims of American sailors that they were not British. The impressment of American seamen without (or even with) their protection certificates became so common that it was one of the justifications for the American declaration of war in 1812.

In 1859, Holmes, as an old man, described his early career and impressment to his nephew, the Reverend Frederic Denison, who carefully transcribed the story.[2] Jeremiah Holmes first went to sea in 1800 at the age of 18. On July 2, 1804, he arrived at the island of St. Helena, in the South Atlantic off Africa, after a French privateer captured the American whaler he had been sailing on. Having lost the protection certificate that verified his American citizenship, Holmes was pressed on board the British 64-gun ship of the line *Trident*. In his words: "When taken aboard *Trident* I was called up for examination by the first lieutenant. I at once said: 'I am an American.' He responded: 'Well, we will make an Englishman of you.' I answered: 'No, sir; you will never do that.'

Holmes wrote to the American consul in London and to family and friends in America, to obtain documents showing that he was an American citizen. The British found the papers insufficient. Holmes began scheming to run away from the British, especially after an incident on board HMS *Saturn* in 1806, when he was put in irons for hitting a British sailor who had said Holmes was "no American, but some nobleman's bastard or else a runaway." When the ship lay off Gibraltar, Holmes tried

As British ships threatened Stonington on August 9, 1814, the defenders of the village turned to these two 18-pound cannons, which had been manufactured in Salisbury, Connecticut, in 1781. Hauled out of storage and placed behind a breastwork on the west side of Stonington Point along with one smaller cannon, they opposed more than 160 cannons on the British attacking ships. Despite a shortage of gunpowder, local volunteers and militia used them to discourage landing parties, score a number of direct hits on HMS *Dispatch*, and contribute to the eventual withdrawal of the British squadron. In 1876 they were formally transferred to the Borough of Stonington by the federal government and placed in a park now known as Cannon Square.

(Courtesy of Mystic Seaport, Mystic, CT; Photographer: Dennis Murphy)

to swim to land at night. When the current changed, he was barely able to make it back to the *Saturn* and climb aboard unseen in the darkness. Back in England, he again applied to the American consul in London, but the British found the consul's papers insufficient because they had "not been ceremoniously endorsed by a regular custom-house officer."

On board a British ship at Portsmouth, England in November 1806, Holmes showed the ship's first lieutenant "certain papers that I had received from Stonington, my native town, signed by the selectmen of the town, certifying my American birth and rights." Holmes told the officer, "yet I am denied my rights. I ought to be discharged. And if I am not set at liberty, I am resolved never more to work for the British crown, let the consequences be what they may." Soon afterwards, Holmes managed without authorization to board an American ship whose mate happened to be acquainted with Stonington. Holmes took a stagecoach to

London, where the American consul had his clerk issue protection papers to Holmes, who sailed back to the U.S. on an American merchant ship. As Holmes put it: "The more I rejoiced in my liberty and my endorsed rights the more I scorned and hated the English that had so long wronged me of my time and strength. And I was glad too that for my liberty I owed the haughty crown no thanks."

On American shore, Holmes "made no delay in finding old Stonington. . . . My experiences had taught me to prize freedom." Because the embargo had crippled American trade with Europe, Holmes went into the coasting trade, continuing even after the war began and British warships began patrolling the East Coast in the summer of 1812. Given the risk of capture by British blockaders, this was a dangerous business, particularly for Holmes, whom the British might well view as a deserter. In 1813, in command of the "famous sloop *Hero*"—in which he was a 25 percent owner—

he managed to elude a British squadron and deliver freight to Charleston, South Carolina, and to make it back to the Mystic River, despite pursuit by a British frigate and a brig.

From his base in Mystic, Holmes also helped battle the British naval squadron that had bottled up Commodore Decatur's squadron in the Thames River. In June 1813 he led the small crew of Mystic mariners who loaded the fishing smack *Charleston* with a cannon and small arms to defend the coasting sloop *Victory*, stranded off Mason's Island in the Mystic River. They transferred their weapons to the *Victory* and drove off two attacks by Btitish barges. In March 1814, Holmes commanded the row galley *Young Hornet* during several unsuccessful nighttime attempts to blow up British warships off New London with torpedoes, so that Decatur's squadron might escape to sea. Holmes also applied his gunnery skills as commander of the three-gun battery constructed on Pistol Point, opposite Fort Rachel, to defend Mystic from attack by British barges.[3]

In July 1814 Admiral Sir Alexander Cochrane, in charge of all the British ships blockading America, ordered them to "lay waste to such towns and districts upon the coast as you may find assailable." That order led to the British attack on Stonington a month later.[4]

At sunrise on 10 August—12 hours after the British attack began—Jeremiah Holmes arrived at Stonington. Some of the hottest action in the three-day struggle was unfolding at that time, and his skills in gunnery and leadership were put to particularly good use. Under his direction the single 18-pounder left in the breastwork repeatedly hulled HMS *Dispatch*, killing two men and wounding 12. The damage done to the enemy brig while the gun was under Holmes's steady command ultimately led Captain Hardy to order the badly leaking *Dispatch* to withdraw from the battle.[5] In that way, Holmes repaid the Royal Navy, "not without some success . . . in the borough of Stonington."

After the war, Holmes continued a maritime career as a successful ship captain and ship owner. Revered as a local hero in Stonington, he lived to be 90, dying on September 14, 1872.

This 18-pound iron cannonball, fired by the British during the Battle of Stonington, landed in the Old Trumbull House in the village. Likely crashing through the roof, it shattered this hearthstone on impact. It survives as a reminder of the dangers of the attack, which placed Stonington's citizens and their property in harm's way.

(Courtesy of Stonington Historical Society, 2009.500.0044)

On the morning of the 10th, Stonington Point had *not* fallen to the British. But now the *Despatch* [*sic*] was warping up the attack. She took a position near the *Terror*, within half a mile of the battery, and anchoring with springs on her cable, at sunrise opened her broadside upon the town, the bomb-ship at the same time emitting shells and carcases [*sic*] in befitting accompaniment.

This was the trying time of the siege. It seemed impossible for any living being to stand within the reach of that fire. But the veterans at the battery remained undaunted till their powder gave out. Their flag was shot down, the breast-work shattered, the earth torn up around them, shells were bursting on all sides, but they left their post only through failure of ammunition. Spiking their single gun, they slowly retired. It is said when the fire from the battery ceased, the crew of the *Despatch* [*sic*] sent their taunts over the water: "We want balls; can't you spare us a few?" To which our men replied, "When the powder comes, you shall have enough."

Eyewitnesses have told us how these men looked in their retreat. Some were without hats and all with garments slouching, tattered, or begrimed. Their faces were blackened with smoke and powder, their muscles strained, eyes burning deep, and hair widely scattered.

For nearly an hour the enemy continued to pour into the village grape shot, 32 lb. cannon, and various combustible and explosive engines used in bombardment without any opposition or annoyance whatever. Drafts of militia men alone remained to patrol the streets and extinguish the fires of any should be kindled.

At 8 o'clock a supply of powder arrived from New London and the 20 volunteers being now refreshed and recruited with 7 or 8 additional braves returned without delay to the battery, drilled out their cannon, nailed their flag to the staff, and renewed the contest.

And now commenced the single-handed action between the 18-pounder and the brig which continued till noon with unremitting fury. The *Despatch* [*sic*] lost a number of her crew and was seriously damaged in hull and rigging. At length, having received several shot below the water line, she slipped her cable and drew off with both pumps going and her deck strewed with ruin. Had not a favorable turn of the wind at that juncture enabled her to escape, she probably would have been abandoned by the crew.

Loud was the shout of victory from all the neighboring hills and militia stations, as well as from the town itself, when the brig retired, crippled and shorn of her glory. The joyful volunteers leaped upon posts and fences, swinging their hats on high and sending after the enemy loud cries of defiance and exultation. Their flag, though pierced with seven shot holes, still waved its folds above them.

Yet they also had suffered. Two of their number had been wounded. One was led away by his companions and the other borne in their arms. Frederick Denison, a youth of 19, one of the bravest of the brave, was struck in the knee by a fragment of rock, and John Miner, also youthful and gallant, was burnt in the face by a premature discharge of the gun. These misfortunes were scarcely realized

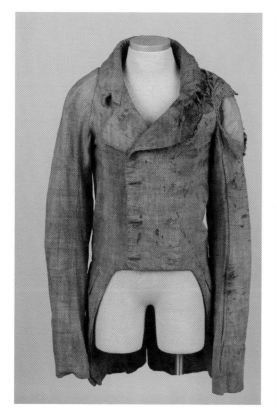

This homemade coat in militia style was worn by 19-year-old militiaman John Miner during the Battle of Stonington. While serving with the gun crew for one of the defenders' 18-pound cannons, he was seriously injured by an explosion. One hundred years later his son described the event: *"I have heard my father say due to the haste and excitement of the volunteers they failed to properly cool their gun before pouring into its muzzle the powder, which due to the excessive heat of the gun caused the powder to explode prematurely, as you may see by reference to the coat— burned and torn upon the neck and shoulder."*

(Coat and letter, courtesy of Stonington Historical Society, 2009.120.001)

at first in the great triumph of the Spartan band. These wounds were at first considered slight. But that of Mr. Denison afterwards developed alarming symptoms, and he expired in October. Mr. Miner remained for a long time totally blind and never recovered the sight of but one eye.

Yet brief was the space that could be given to rejoicing. The *Ramillies* was soon observed coming to avenge the defeat of her comrades. Leaving her distant post of observation, she approached as near as her draught of water would permit and seemed determined to demolish the village. The *Pactolus* also drew up and anchored by her side.

The fate of Stonington now seemed decided. Yet the magistrates resolved upon making one more effort to save it. A flag was dispatched to Sir Thomas Hardy with Mess'rs Lord and Williams, an honorable deputation from their number, to state their anxiety to preserve their village and enquire what was his determination respecting it.

These gentlemen were detained an hour and then returned with a written communication from the Commodore of very extraordinary import. It stated that the deputation having assured him that no torpedoes had been fitted out from Stonington, and engaging to use their influence that none should be hereafter, if Mrs. Stewart, wife of James Stewart, Esq., late H. M. Consul at New London was sent on board the *Ramillies* by 8 o'clock the next morning, no further hostilities would be committed against the town; otherwise it would be thoroughly destroyed.

This ultimatum was received with surprise, contempt, and indignation. No torpedoes had been fitted out from Stonington, and no project of the kind had been entertained by the inhabitants. The only torpedo enterprise that had been undertaken in Long Island Sound since the commencement of the war was that of the *Eagle*, a small fire ship that had exploded near the *Ramillies* June 25th, 1813. But this was fitted out from New York, and the people of Connecticut had no concern in it.*

Of Mrs. Stewart and her family, the inhabitants of Stonington had no control whatever. When Mr. Stewart privately withdrew from the country and retired on board the British fleet, he left his family at New London, where they were subsequently detained by order of the general government—restricted from leaving the country but otherwise entirely at liberty. Mrs. Stewart has been uniformly treated with respect and attention by the principal inhabitants, both of New London and Stonington. No fear for her personal safety could have prompted this demand, which was the more extraordinary as the memorial of Mr. Stewart asking permission for his family to join him on board the British squadron had been received by General Cushing and transmitted to the proper authorities at Washington. There was no doubt but that the request would be granted, but time for action on it had not yet been allowed.

At 8 o'clock the next morning, the hour fixed by Commodore Hardy for the expiration of the truce, the magistrates sent a flag to the squadron, briefly stating their inability to comply with his requisitions. To their note a verbal answer was returned by the Commodore that he would wait until 12 o'clock and if Mrs. Stewart was not brought on board by that time he should proceed to demolish the town.

In accordance with this threat the bombardment was renewed in the afternoon by the *Terror*, which took her station where she could not be reached by the cannon from the battery, and continued her fiery discharge upon the town until evening. No opposition could be made, and all force was withdrawn from the place, by Brigadier General Isham, the officer in command, except a guard of militia that patrolled the streets to extinguish fires.

The third night of the siege was allowed to pass in silence, but at an early hour the next morning [Friday, August 12] the fiery shower of bombs and rockets was renewed. At 8 o'clock the *Ramillies* and *Pactolus* having worked their way still nearer to the Point, opened a heavy cannonade with the design of raking the village and sweeping it, as it were, from the earth. But the rocks and shallows of the deep prevented this project. The roar was tremendous, and the cannonade long continued, but most of the balls either fell short or passed over the Point.

While this tremendous cannonade was at its height, a very hazardous service was performed by a volunteer band of the Norwich artillery under the command of Lt. Lathrop. In execution of an order from the commanding officer they marched through the village to the battery and dragged the cannon from thence to the north end of the point, that it might be serviceable, if an attempt should be made to land under cover of the ships. This exploit was performed without accident, though the party were exposed during the whole time to the enemy's fire. (Some say the service was performed by volunteers from Col. Belcher's regiment under ensigns Gallop and Bellows, but this is probably a mistake. Lieut. Augustus Lathrop (afterwards Capt.) was of Norwich town and was certainly engaged in this exploit. Charles Gale, one of his men still living, often speaks of it.)

The cannonade ceased about noon, and the ships, baffled in their attempts to destroy the town hauled off to their former anchorage. The next morning, August 13th, they weighed anchor and returned to their usual station off New London harbor.

The bombardment had been kept up with intervals of cessation to the 4th day, commencing

*Ms. Caulkins, in 1828, was seemingly uninformed of other attempts on the British fleet by American "destructive machines," which are detailed in chapter 3.

on Tuesday August 9th and ceasing at noon August 12th. On the American side six persons in all had been wounded, but most of them slightly. Lieut. Hough of the drafted militia was very active during the siege, and one of the wounded. About 40 buildings were more or less injured, but none so shattered as not to be easily repaired. A horse and one or two other domestic animals were killed. The whole damage was estimated at $3,500.

The loss of the British in men was stated at 21 men killed and upwards of 50 wounded. (Holmes, *Annals*, vol. 2, 466.) The damage to their brig and small craft was very serious and their waste of the engines of war enormous. It was estimated that they fired 50 tons of metal into the place. The larger carcases [*sic*] filled with combustibles were marked with the weight 218 lbs. One of these missiles for many years adorned the summit of a gate post in the village bearing the inscription "Bomb-ship Terror, Aug. 10th, 1814, W. 215 lb." On the other side, "Stonington will be defended while its heroes have one cannon ball."

Familiarity soon diminishes the sense of danger. The Congreve rockets at first filled the inhabitants with dismay. A vague idea of their explosive power caused an exaggerated fear of their effects, but when it was found that they did but little damage, they lost their terror and were despised as falling short of their reputation. It was wonderful with what coolness the guard would patrol the streets while the cannon balls were whizzing over their heads and shells ands bombs clattering upon the roofs or sinking into the earth before them. During the first night of the attack some few persons remained in town as a guard against plunderers, the inhabitants not having had time to remove their effects. One man had promised a widow woman that he would take special care of her house. After the firing ceased, he went into it and lay down, soon falling into a sleep from which he was only aroused by the recommencement of the bombardment the next morning. He ran out to look around and see the state of affairs, but soon returning found the bed that he had just left rolled into a tumultuous heap, smoking and steaming with sulphur, a bomb or shell deeply ensconced in the center among the feathers. It had descended through the roof but was smothered in the bed. The veterans of the battery would often expose themselves to the enemy's fire with cool, insulting bravado. One of these in the early part of the attack, boldly passed from one gun to the other upon the platform seven times in succession, and every time the enemy fired, he waved his hat and shouted derisively. But this was an efflux of over-wrought excitement, not the calm courage that merits applause.

When the village was first cleared of its inhabitants on the evening of August 9th, there was but one person found too feeble to be removed. This was an aged and infirm widow, almost in a dying condition, the spark of life burning so feebly that an attempt to convey her from the house would probably extinguish the flame at once. An affectionate daughter, the only one of her mother, undismayed at the danger to which she was exposed, remained by her side.

The house was near the battery, at the center of confusion and uproar. The earth trembled under them and sulphurous fires inflamed the heavens. Buildings around were shattered; a furious bomb burst through the roof of the very house in which they were, but filial affection kept its post, soothing the restlessness of disease and administering to the last wants of dissolving nature. While the cannonade raged like a tempest on the second day of the siege, the spirit passed away, and Huldah Hall, having caught the last words of earthly love and Christian hope of her beloved parent, closed her rayless eyes and sat down by her side to watch the dear remains.

At an interval in the bombardment the soldiers came in to perform the rotes of sepulcher. The straw pallet was taken from her bed, the body laid upon it and covered with a counterpane. It was then borne by the four corners in solemn silence to the grave-yard, with the patient daughter as sole mourner walking by its side. Just where they would have prepared the grave, a falling bomb had rent the earth and lay embedded in the cavity. Hastily they disinterred the steaming ball and laid their burden in its place. The funeral service was read and the remains decently covered with earth. The roar of the enemy's cannonade was the deep organ music that assisted in these solemn rites.

"Preserved upon no historic page and emblazoned on no splendid monument is the name of Huldah Hall—but in the records which the household gods keep is a leaf that immortalizes this humble individual for one of the most beautiful examples of filial love." M. E. Wentworth

The real object of the British in the attack upon Stonington has never been made clear. The plea of the torpedoes and the demand for Mrs. Stewart were all the reasons alleged, but these were trivial in the extreme, and brought forward perhaps partly as pretexts for relinquishing the assault and sparing the place. It was an act of aggression wholly at variance with the known character of Sir Thomas Hardy. In fact he had assured the deputation that waited upon him from the village that it was the most unpleasant expedition in which he had ever been engaged. He was willing to have it understood that he acted under orders from his superiors.

Partly from the difficulty of accounting for this act on any other supposition, a deep-laid plan of operations was at the time attributed to the British commander.

It was supposed that the object of the attack upon Stonington was to draw the military force of the neighborhood to that point—then to sail up the Mystic River, land a large force at the Head, march one detachment to Norwich and take possession of that place, and another to Groton, which would come upon the rear of Fort Griswold and take that fortress by storm; thus having command of the two extremities of the Thames, the United States ships then lying in the river would fall easy prey and New London itself might be either occupied or laid under contribution.

General Cushing's defensive measures were adapted to meet these suppositions. Acting in concert with Major General Williams of the militia, several regiments were called out and strong detachments stationed at the four chief points supposed to be threatened—Stonington, Mystic, Norwich, and New London.

But only the initial step, the bombardment of Stonington, was ever undertaken, nor has anything since been disclosed that would verify the supposed scheme. The force they had upon the coast was totally inadequate to a project of such magnitude; and before it could be accomplished, they might reasonably expect that half of New London would be rushing down upon them, with a power sufficient to hurl them into the sea.

The whole affair coincides so exactly with the system of operations pursued by Admiral Cochrane at the south that we may venture to refer it to the same plan, and account for it in the same way. Admiral Cochrane, Vice-Admiral of the Sea, arrived on the coast August 3, clothed with paramount authority over the naval force in America, and issuing orders to all under his command "to destroy and lay waste such towns and districts on the coast as might be found assailable." This was the main feature of his policy, grounded upon a plea of retaliation for ravages committed by the army of the United States in Upper Canada. No such ravages however had ever been authorized or countenanced by the American Government, but on the contrary had been severely reprehended and the conduct of the officers allowing it subjected to judicial investigation and censure.

FRANCES MANWARING CAULKINS, 1828

The Reverend as Barometer:
Connecticut's Conflicting Views of the War of 1812
written by Meredith Mason Brown

DIFFERENT SECTIONS OF AMERICA had widely contrasting views of the War of 1812— so much so that the fledgling Union was at risk. The newer western states (notably Kentucky, Tennessee, and Ohio) largely favored the war with Great Britain as a way to eliminate the remaining Indian threat. Connecticut and other New England states, however, generally disapproved of the war. They had seen their trade with Europe and the Caribbean drop significantly as a result of President Jefferson's 1807 embargo on foreign commerce. This was followed by a short-term rebound, but by 1812, trade had been reduced to a trickle as a result of the British and French restrictions and shifting American policies. Some trade from New England continued indirectly through Canada—trade that Britain, needing American goods to carry on the Napoleonic wars in Europe, encouraged by largely exempting New England from the naval blockade in the first two years of the war. The war looked likely to stifle America's overseas commerce even more, because of America's direct conflict with Britain and the likelihood of American invasions of Canada. This prospect was grim not only for those living in coastal New England towns like New Haven and Stonington, but also for those in the New England interior, because they would not be able to buy goods from overseas, or to have their own goods sold abroad. Yet, by the fall of 1814 some residents of maritime Connecticut were increasingly supportive of the war, in large part because the British by that time were patrolling Long Island Sound and attacking coastal towns. This change of view

did not necessarily occur in other parts of the state.

The evolving views of the Reverend Ira Hart illustrate changing attitudes towards the war. Pastor of the First Congregational Church in Stonington from 1809 until his death in 1829, Hart was an intelligent and well-read Yale graduate. He preached strongly against the war soon after it started, but he also rallied round the flag when the British attacked his town. In some measure, Hart can be seen as a barometer for Connecticut's conflicting views of the war.

The U.S. declared war against Britain in June of 1812. The weakness of Congress's approval of the declaration reflected America's ambivalence about what many critics referred as "Mr. Madison's War": the House vote to approve was 78 to 49; the Senate's, 19 to 13. No Federalists voted for the declaration. On June 30, both houses of Congress requested that Madison recommend a day "of public humiliation and prayer to be observed by the people of the United States, with religious solemnity, and the offering of fervent supplications to the Almighty God" for "the speedy restoration of peace." Madison tried to make the occasion one that would build up nationwide support for the war. In his July 9 proclamation recommending such a day, he referred to "the injustice of a foreign government" which had involved the United States in the war, and recommended the American people make supplications to God to "animate their patriotism, and bestow His blessing on their arms."[1]

The sermon preached by Ira Hart on August 16 responded to Madison's proclamation, but—

After hostilities ended, Midshipman Powers received a proper tombstone in Stonington's Evergreen Cemetery: "Here rest the remains of Mr. Thomas Barratt Powers, aged 18 years. Late Midshipman of H.B. Majesty's Ship Superb, who was killed in action in a boat on the 31st July 1814: a Native of Market Bosworth in the County of Leicestershire England." A side panel notes, "This Memorial was erected by the Honble Captn Paget, and his Brother Officers as a tribute of respect and esteem."

(Courtesy of Mystic Seaport, Mystic, CT; Photographer: Dennis Murphy)

like comparable sermons being preached at about the same time elsewhere in New England—in a way that encouraged his congregation to support the war no more than the Constitution required. Hart began by urging Americans with differing views of the war not to slander each other. He chose as his text Acts 7, verse 26: "Sirs Ye are Brethren; why do ye wrong one to another?" Noting that "real injury may be done by invidious names and terms of reproach," he asked, "Where is the liberty of thought, Speech or action, if a man may not express in a decent manner the sober convictions of his Judgment without being called a Tory." His pained question suggested that he had been criticized as a Tory—a supporter of Britain, rather than a loyal American—for questioning the wisdom and morality of the war.[2]

Hart preached that Americans were "unjustly engaged in a State of warfare," but added: "Those who disapprove of the war—still must be good citizens, must resort to none but constitutional means of redress—They must therefore render all that assistance to the government, wh[ich] they have promised in the national compact." In this declaration, Hart, like many in New England at the time, appears to be invoking the Constitution as a basis for limiting the support to be given to the war. The Constitution—Article I, section 8—empowers Congress to "provide for calling forth the Militia to execute the Laws of the Union, suppress Insurrections, and repel Invasions." Connecticut and other New England states read this to mean that Congress could not require the state militia to be placed under the command of federal officers and to be sent to fight in Canada, since (at least in 1812) there had been no "invasion" (or insurrection, or breaking of federal law). In fact, in 1812, Connecticut (like Rhode Island, New Hampshire, and Vermont) refused to send its militia into federal service, although requested to do so by President Madison.[3] While noting the obligation of Americans to comply

with the Constitution, Hart also said, "But no government has a right to decree injustice, or to dissolve that moral obligation [to love one another, to do unto others as you would have done unto you] wh[ich] G[od] has ordained."

Two years later, responding vehemently to an unauthorized American raid that destroyed businesses and houses in Long Point, Ontario, Sir Alexander Cochrane, the admiral in charge of all British ships on the east coast of America, on July 18, 1814, issued an order directing all those ships "to destroy and lay waste such towns and districts upon the coast as you find assailable." That order led to British attacks in Maine and, in August, on Stonington, Connecticut. Before that latter attack, on July 30, 1814, Captain Charles Paget, in charge of the 74-gun HMS *Superb*, sent a barge commanded by 18-year-old Midshipman Thomas Barratt Powers to inspect a vessel near the end of Long Island that turned out to be a heavily armed American privateer. Although Powers removed his hat to show that he was surrendering, someone on the privateer shot him through the head. That night the privateer's captain sailed to Stonington, delivered the captured barge and the dead Powers to the militia at Stonington, then sailed off in the darkness. Stonington officials were understandably concerned that the British would suspect that Stonington, having Powers's body, must have been involved in his killing. Rev. Hart, who was also the chaplain of the 30th Regiment of the 3rd Brigade of the Connecticut militia, arranged for the midshipman's burial in Stonington Cemetery with full military honors. In the event, Paget did not blame Stonington for the death; instead, he and his fellow officers subscribed the money for a monument over Powers's grave. That monument still stands in the Stonington Cemetery.[4]

Less than two weeks after the killing of Powers, on August 9, 1814, the gun-laden British squadron commanded by Captain Sir Thomas

Masterman Hardy was bombarding Stonington, implementing Admiral Cochrane's July 18 order. The British attack on Stonington was a form of invasion of Connecticut, which under the Constitution gave the president of the United States the power to call out the Connecticut militia. Without waiting for a presidential order, the Connecticut militia (including Rev. Hart) came out in force—not only from Stonington, but also from Groton and New London— because their neighborhood was being threatened. The British naval attacks in 1814 on Stonington, Pettipauge, and other Connecticut towns—coupled with Britain's 1814 extension of its blockade to previously exempt New England—changed the attitudes of some in Connecticut towards the war. That said, the recalcitrance of native New Englanders led President Madison to write to a friend as late as November of 1814 that "the conduct of our eastern states was the source of our greatest difficulties in carrying on the war," and that most in that part of the country "have been brought by their leaders, aided by their priests, under a delusion scarcely exceeded by that region in the period of witchcraft."[5]

Madison's view would be strengthened when Connecticut Federalists at the Hartford Convention expressed their hatred of the war. Hart in his August 16, 1812, sermon had said, "I can see but one justifiable cause of war & that is self-defence." During the Battle of Stonington, perhaps motivated by self-defense, there were enough militiamen defending or near the borough of Stonington to dissuade Hardy from another attempt to land British Royal Marines on the point—though the British bombardment continued sporadically through that day. Hart, too, was at the battle, as part of the militia, since he was the chaplain of the 30th regiment.

Rev. Hart, however, also evidently bore in mind broad Christian principles reflected in his August 16, 1812, sermon, the teaching of Christ to "love your enemies = They are brethren of the human family == A state of war does not cancel this obligation." Four British had died on the morning of August 10, 1814, when Stonington's defenders managed to sink a barge full of Royal Marines bound for Stonington Point. As Amos Palmer, chairman of Stonington's committee of defense, put it in a letter to American Secretary of War William Crawford, "We took up and buried four poor fellows that were hove overboard out of the sinking barge." Although there is no evidence to prove the case, it is likely that Ira Hart, minister of the community's Congregational Church, officiated at that burial, too. His compassion was also expressed in 1815 when young Thomas Powers's father came from England to Stonington to see his son's grave. It was Reverend Hart, a Connecticut Yankee who had consistently spoken his conscience, who took the elder Powers to the grave and commiserated with him.[6]

The Battle of Goshen Point
A Victory for "Jefferson's Gunboats"

written by Andrew W. German

THE US NAVY WAS LAUNCHED with a few large warships to represent the nation and its interests on the high seas. But when the navy engaged in its first distant-water war, against Tripoli, small gunboats became necessary to operate effectively alongshore. The success of nine small gunboats, which made the voyage to North Africa and back, gave President Thomas Jefferson the impression that the navy could defend the nation's isolationist aims more economically with gunboats than with frigates. During the Jefferson and Madison administrations, the navy commissioned 174 gunboats between 1805 and 1812.

The gunboats were built to a number of designs, but generally they measured about 50 feet in length and 18 in beam, with a shallow draft. They were rigged as either two-masted schooners or single-masted sloops, but were also equipped with sweeps (long oars) for maneuvering in light winds or constricted waters. Most were armed with one to three guns: perhaps a 24- or 32-pounder on a swiveling carriage amidships and a smaller gun, or several 18-pounders. They generally had crews of about 40, including 24 seamen and 7 Marines.[1]

During the War of 1812, the 126 gunboats still in service were dispersed among the ports along the Atlantic coast and at New Orleans. Initially laid up, they were put back into service early in 1813 as British forces moved into coastal waters. New London merited two, Gunboats 91 and 92.[2]

At New York, US Navy Commander Jacob Lewis, a former privateer captain, was commodore of the fleet of 53 gunboats. They guarded the Narrows and lower bay, and occasionally patrolled to the eastward through the East River and Hell Gate into Long Island Sound. Shortly after he was bottled up at New London, Commodore Decatur even suggested that Lewis bring 25 gunboats east to surround Sir Thomas Hardy's 74-gun HMS *Ramillies* at low tide and capture her, a proposal rejected by the secretary of the navy.[3]

New London's two gunboats appear to have been kept in reserve for defensive purposes within the harbor. In March 1814, Commodore Decatur had them anchored in the narrows of the Thames River off Winthrop Point to deter any British attempt to reach the squadron at Gales Ferry.

However, the New York gunboat flotilla became a regular presence on the Sound as the British warships and their barges began to roam at will. In August 1813, *Niles' Register* reported: "A division of the New-York flotilla of gunboats, under com. *Lewis*, is now in *Long Island Sound*.—They check the operations of the enemy's barges, and prevent an abominable trade and intercourse with him."[4] Eleven of the gunboats ventured within four miles of New London, accompanying a merchant brig and schooner. As Sylvanus Griswold noted in his journal on August 4: "the New York Squadron appears of[f]–4 mile . . . 1 brig 1 schooner & 11 gunboats [British] ships send 5 barges half [way] across the Sound to v[i]ew our fleet 1 gunboat stood for them fired a gun distance 3 miles & home they fled."[5]

Commodore Lewis's flotilla made its greatest contribution in May 1814. With the

Nova Scotia privateer *Liverpool Packet* cruising in the Sound, Lewis led 13 gunboats through Hell Gate to drive her away. Along the way they called at Black Rock, New Haven, and Saybrook. There, 40 coasters, including Captain Howard's New London packet *Juno*, huddled for protection from British barges. When they prevailed on Lewis to convoy them safely to New London, he pointed out that gunboats were no match for a frigate, but agreed to try.[6]

Off Goshen Point (now Harkness Park in Waterford), the frigate *Maidstone*, sloop of war *Sylph*, and a sloop attempted to block their passage. According to the *Connecticut Gazette*:

> The wind being extremely light, the frigate was compelled to come to, and the *Sylph* fled under her protection. After passing to the leeward of the enemy under a constant and rapid fire, Com. Lewis endeavoured to work his boats to the windward of the ships, in which six only succeeded. The firing continued from about 6 o'clock till past 8 in the evening, when the squadron of gun boats came to anchor in the mouth of our harbor. One of the boats [Number 6] received a shot between wind and water, and was run ashore to stop the leak, which was speedily effected. And a seaman had a leg badly fractured by the recoiling of a gun. No other damage was sustained on our part. What damage the enemy received, if any, in our opinion remains to be divulged, although reports tell of 15 men having been killed on board the *Maidstone*, and that she was essentially injured in her spars and rigging. It is calculated that 1500 cannon balls were fired in the contest.[7]

Their work done and repairs made, the gunboats returned to the westward, and Lewis reported that the British "appeared unwilling to renew the action the following morning," leading him to conclude the *Maidstone* had indeed suffered significant casualties.[8]

Gunboats would also perform valuable service during the British effort to take New Orleans. The small naval squadron there included six gunboats, which initially patrolled the approaches to the port. In the summer of 1814 they raided the pirate lair of Jean Lafitte in Barataria Bay. Late in 1814, five of the gunboats under Lieutenant Thomas ap Catesby Jones were sent to Lake Borgne, east of New Orleans, to prevent the British advance up the shallow lake. On December 14 the gunboats were arrayed across the lake when 42 British barges, with more than 1,000 men, attacked them. Twice the gunboats drove the barges back, and inflicted greater casualties than they received, before they were overwhelmed and captured by the British. Nevertheless, the gunboats helped delay the British approach on New Orleans and helped galvanize the defenders, including some of Lafitte's men, who stood with Andrew Jackson at Chalmette on January 8.[9]

"Jefferson's gunboats" have usually been considered a failure reflective of President Jefferson's ineffective naval policy. But during the War of 1812, these gunboats performed valuable service on a number of occasions—particularly at Goshen Point and Lake Borgne.

British Barges and Yankee Tricks

written by Andrew W. German

WHILE THE BRITISH 74s normally took station between New London and Montauk Point, the frigates and sloops of war cruised the coast, making regular patrols all the way up Long Island Sound. But the most effective British patrol vessels were the barges carried by the warships. The second-largest of a warship's boats, a barge was usually 36 feet long and was propelled by either sails or 12 oars. Armed with muskets and cutlasses and sometimes a swivel gun, and large enough to carry a complement of Royal Marines, a barge could threaten lightly defended shore installations or overtake and capture coasting vessels in the Sound.

The attack on Pettipauge was the most audacious of the barge adventures, but even as commerce on the Sound slowed to a trickle, almost every week the newspapers reported the seizure of one or more coasting vessels by barges. "The *petit guerre* of the Sound has been extremely lively for the last week," reported the *Connecticut Gazette* at the beginning of May 1814. "Wednesday last a sloop from New York, Forsyth, master, belonging here, was chased on shore near Mill-Stone, and abandoned by the crew; leaving a Mrs. Howard of this place, and an English woman passengers on board. The barges took off the last, and left Mrs. H. It was apparent the enemy intended the destruction of the vessel and cargo; but in consequence of the urgent intreaty and distressing situation of Mrs. H. they left the vessel as they found her."

A few weeks later three barges chased the New London packet *Mary* into Niantic Bay and right up against the Rope Ferry Bridge, which caught fire when they burned the vessel. The

paper announced, "The British barges have been for several days skulking under the western shore, to intercept vessels taking the inner channel; which makes it extremely dangerous to attempt making this harbor or Fisher's Island sound, without a very strong wind."[1]

Occasionally the barges fell victim to "Yankee tricks." In August 1814, after two unsuccessful barge assaults on the "cursed little hornet's nest" of Mystic, some Mystic men played a lethal trick. With the British bomb vessel *Terror* anchored off the Dumplings, just across Fishers Island Sound, the local militia hid themselves near the shore on Groton Long Point and on Morgan Point. Simeon Haley, captain of the private armed boat *True Blooded Yankee* of Mystic, and a crew of four then manned a large fishing boat and made their way into the Sound to tempt the British. The *Terror*'s sailing master took command of a barge and set out after the Mystic boat, which ran in toward Groton Long Point. As the barge reached the shore to capture the boat, the militia rose up and fired, killing one, wounding two, and capturing the other 12 men. Lieutenant Chambers, the captured sailing master commented, "I have heard of Yankee tricks, but this is the first that I have experienced."[2]

Among the most active patriots in the "cursed little hornet's nest" of Mystic was Captain Simeon Haley (1781-1859). Haley went to sea at 17 and was captain by 23. In 1813, he was part of the crew from Mystic that saved the sloop *Victory* from capture, and he acted as prize master of the privateer *Hero*, taking command of the *Fox* after her capture by the *Hero*. During the Battle of Stonington Haley served in the battery, frequently being the one to fire the cannon. Haley also commanded the private armed boat *True Blooded Yankee*, as well as the boat that lured a British barge to capture at Groton Long Point. This postwar painting is attributed to John Brewster Jr. (© Mystic Seaport Collection, Mystic, CT, #1941.265)

CHAPTER FIVE

An End to the War

NEGOTIATIONS BETWEEN THE TWO WARRING POWERS began early in 1814 with mutual agreement to seek a diplomatic solution. But Napoleon's defeat in April released the full might of the British Empire to deal with the US. When the peace commissioners began meeting in Ghent, Belgium, in early August of 1814, the American delegation was filled with the talents of Albert Gallatin, John Quincy Adams, and their colleagues. However, without the French threat on Great Britain's doorstep, British negotiators felt little pressure to offer any diplomatic concessions to the Americans. Early negotiations were stalled by the British demands for the protection of Indian lands in nearly all of the Northwest Territory. The Americans, who had won hard-fought victories in that region, and who lusted after native lands, refused.

In support of its position, American fortunes at sea in 1814 had continued with mixed results. After refitting at Nukahiva in the Marquesas Islands—which Captain David Porter considered annexing for the United States—the frigate *Essex* and her converted whaleships were blockaded and defeated by the Royal Navy at Valparaiso, Chile, on March 28. The *Constitution* had made a short cruise to the West Indies at the beginning of 1814, but she had to return to Boston for repairs in March and would spend the rest of the year blockaded there. The USS *President* had cruised the Atlantic and North Sea through 1813, taking a few prizes, but she had been blockaded at New York since February 1814. Her consort through much of 1812 and 1813, the USS *Congress*, had made a South Atlantic cruise before returning to Portsmouth, New Hampshire, at the end of 1813. She was laid up there through 1814. Connecticut Captain Charles Morris, formerly Hull's lieutenant in the *Constitution*, took command of the sloop of war *Adams* and escaped the Chesapeake Bay in January 1814, making two Atlantic cruises after merchant prizes before he withdrew into the Penobscot River for repairs in the fall.

On the northern border, the British had crossed the Niagara River, captured Fort Niagara, and burned Buffalo at the end of 1813. To maintain its domination of Lakes Erie and Ontario, the US Navy sent men from saltwater ships, including the USS *Macedonian*, to the Lakes. Both sides were building 74-gun ships of the line there.

The attack on Stonington in August of 1814 was a small part of the larger, loosely coordinated British military strategy to weaken America around the edges, either to have the US sue for peace or to strengthen the British bargaining position at the negotiations in Ghent. With the defeat of Napoleon, 16,000 British troops were committed to service against the US. The overall plan called for a forceful naval effort to spread fear among weakly defended coastal communities, and a return to Chesapeake Bay to capture the nation's capital and the privateering center of Baltimore. There would also be a drive south from Canada along Lake Champlain to isolate New England (as attempted unsuccessfully during the Revolutionary War), and a drive up the Mississippi River to capture the strategic port of New Orleans through which Western commerce flowed to the sea. Full success would defeat the US; partial success would significantly weaken America's negotiating position in the search for peace.

On the far eastern border of Massachusetts (now Maine), Captain Hardy and the *Ramillies* led an expedition that seized Eastport in mid-July without firing a shot. He was back in Connecticut waters for the bombardment of Stonington a month later, before heading south to join the assault in the Chesapeake at the end of August. Off New London, Hardy was replaced by Admiral Henry Hotham and Captain Charles Paget in HMS *Superb*.

Late in August, Sir John Sherbrooke led a British force south from Halifax, Nova Scotia, and captured Machias, Maine. When he learned that Captain Morris had taken the USS *Adams* into the Penobscot River, Sherbrooke came up Penobscot Bay, captured Castine, then sent a force upriver. At Hampden, Morris unshipped his guns to assist the militia in driving off the British boats. When the militia fled before the British regulars, Morris had to blow up the *Adams* and escape across country to Portland. That left the river open to Bangor, which was plundered. Sherbrooke then declared all of Maine east of the Penobscot to be the Canadian province of New Ireland, which it remained until April 1815.

Much like the coast of Maine, the extensive waters of the Chesapeake Bay could be dominated by the power of the Royal Navy. The British campaign in the region began with the seizure of Tangier Island during the first week of April. In May and June, they ranged along the banks of the Patuxent River, raiding and neutralizing Joshua Barney's armed fleet of barges that were charged with protecting the Bay. In July they had raided as far north as Elkton, Maryland, but larger targets were in their sights.

The campaign to capture Washington, DC, began on August 19. After overwhelming the disorganized American force at Bladensburg on August 24, British infantry marched unopposed into the nation's capital. The night and early morning of the following day were illuminated by the fires that destroyed the White House, Capitol, Treasury, and offices of the secretaries of state and of war. Although the British departed so quickly that they left their wounded behind, they had achieved their goal of avenging the destruction of York, the provincial capital of Upper Canada the previous year. At the same time, American morale was dealt its greatest blow as the young nation suffered the ignominy of having its seat of government destroyed.

While the destruction of government buildings in Washington was a serious blow to American morale, the successful defense of the strategic port of Baltimore would eventually attain mythic significance for the American people. The September 12-14 attack on the Chesapeake Bay's largest port, and the nation's center of privateering activity, was two-pronged. The approach by land was blunted early by the loss of the able British commander Robert Ross, who had sacked Washington three weeks earlier. His successor ultimately chose not to assault the formidable American defenses when the expected naval support did not materialize. The ships of the Royal Navy never arrived to

Macdonough's Victory on Lake Champlain.

AND DEFEAT OF THE BRITISH ARMY AT PLATTSBURG BY GEN! MACOMB, SEPT? 11TH 1814.

In the fall of 1814 a British force advanced down Lake Champlain to divide New England from the rest of the US. But a small American naval squadron led by Master Commandant Thomas Macdonough, and a contingent of militia, stood in the way. Aligned with British infantry, Captain George Downie's British squadron entered Plattsburgh Bay on September 11, 1814. Macdonough had anchored his flotilla to intercept the British, adjusting the anchor lines to aim the guns. American fire shattered the British flagship, and the rest of the squadron surrendered or were destroyed. This victory and the repulse of the British on land (background) forced their retreat and negated British claims for territorial acquisition during peace negotiations. This 1816 engraving by Benjamin Tanner is based on a painting by Hugh Reinagle.

(© Mystic Seaport Collection, Mystic, CT, #1961.39)

aid the land troops because they never passed Fort McHenry, just south of Baltimore itself.

The bombardment of Fort McHenry took place over a full day, beginning at 6:00 a.m. on September 13, 1814. When Francis Scott Key saw the nation's colors still flying above the ramparts the following morning, he was inspired to pen his poem, "Defence of Fort McHenry," which began to circulate through America within weeks of the battle. He later set the poem to the tune of a drinking song, which became *The Star Spangled Banner.*

The second prong of the British grand strategy also went into motion at the end of August. To counter that threat, Master Commandant Thomas Macdonough, a former resident of Middletown, Connecticut, commanded a new flotilla of four warships at Otter Creek, Vermont, on Lake Champlain, while a few thousand regulars and militiamen held the opposite side of the lake near Plattsburgh, New York. At Montreal, British Lieutenant General Sir George Prevost planned an invasion on the New York side of the lake to avoid enraging Vermonters. Prevost had a mix of Canadians and British veterans of the Spanish campaign against Napoleon totaling more than 10,000. American forces retired when Prevost reached Plattsburgh, but he waited there until the British flotilla could drive Macdonough out of Plattsburgh Bay, where he had anchored his vessels for maximum firepower and maneuverability. On September 11 the British squadron engaged. The vessels were small—the largest being the HMS *Confiance* with 38 guns and the USS *Saratoga* with 26 guns—but the firing was intense. Within a couple of hours the British commander was dead, the *Confiance* had surrendered, and most of the British gunboats had fled. The remaining British ships surrendered. Without naval support, Prevost withdrew his infantry and returned to Canada. What might seem a minor victory actually

Thomas Macdonough (1783-1825), a native of Delaware, entered the US Navy in 1800, serving with distinction during the Barbary War. He fought alongside Stephen Decatur during their notable raid to destroy the USS *Philadelphia*, which had been captured by the enemy. An assignment to supervise gunboat construction in 1806 brought him to Middletown, Connecticut, where he met and later married Lucy Ann Shaler. Macdonough was placed in command of the US naval squadron on Lake Champlain, and in September 1814 he defeated a British squadron and won national acclaim for his action at Plattsburgh Bay. Macdonough died at sea in 1825 and was buried in his adopted hometown of Middletown.

(© Mystic Seaport Collection, Mystic, CT, #1961.685)

secured the northern frontier and denied British negotiators at Ghent any claim to extending the boundaries of Canada.

British warships still ranged Long Island Sound, and increasing numbers of "Blue Light Federalists" (a reference to the supposed traitors who signaled the British at New London) attempted to trade with them. The US Revenue Cutter *Eagle*, stationed in New Haven took three American vessels that were engaged in this business.[1] In October 1814, the *Eagle's* commander, Captain Frederick Lee, learned that the American schooner *Susan* had been taken off Westport by an armed tender of HMS *Pomone*, and was being taken east down the Sound. Gathering several dozen volunteers from New Haven, Lee gave chase through the night. On the morning of October 10, 1814, Lee found himself not only near his quarry, but also within range of the British brig *Dispatch*, which had suffered so much damage off Stonington.

Lee then followed the common maritime practice when faced with an overwhelming force and ran the *Eagle* as far into shallow water as possible while firing his guns to keep the enemy at bay. She grounded near the mouth of the Wading River on the north shore of Long Island, under what was then known as Negro Head (now Friar's Head), across the Sound from Branford. By the time the *Dispatch* had hauled up to fire on the unfortunate cutter, Lee had abandoned the vessel and moved a number of his cannon to the top of the headland, where he joined forces with local volunteers who had responded to the alarm and were keeping up a fire against the *Dispatch* and her tender. After pounding away at the beached *Eagle* for approximately five hours, the *Dispatch* moved away, leaving the holed American vessel dismasted and full of water.

By early afternoon the following day the *Dispatch* had sailed to Guilford, where she offloaded the passengers from the prize *Susan*. Having battled to keep the *Eagle* from falling into British hands, Captain Lee took advantage of the British departure, patched up his cutter, pumped her dry, and with the help of local men prepared to sail her to safety. Such an effort takes time, however, and she was still there two days later when the *Dispatch* returned in company with HMS *Narcissus* and brought the *Eagle* under their guns once more. In spite of fire from the Americans on the headland, the Royal Navy easily took control of the *Eagle* and towed her out from under the Americans' noses, bound for Plum Island at the eastern end of the Sound.

The spirited defense of the Revenue Cutter *Eagle* is still celebrated by today's US Coast Guard. Her story is a part of that service's tradition, and is commemorated in a mural that can be found in Satterlee Hall at the Coast Guard Academy in New London, as well as in the name of the Coast Guard's signature vessel, the training barque *Eagle*.[2]

The capture of the *Eagle* represents the nature of the protracted conflict in Long Island Sound. Royal Navy power was overwhelming, and it limited the movement of American vessels at will. And yet, American forces, many of them "irregulars," played the shifting, tides, changing visibility, and limited maneuvering room in their determined efforts to protect home waters and property.

The fall of 1814 also saw some American naval successes on salt water. Robert Fulton's steam battery, the USS *Demologos*, was launched at the end of October, and work hurried ahead to make her the world's first steam-powered warship. The first American ship of the line, the 90-gun USS *Independence*, had been completed at Boston and now stood guard at the harbor there. The USS

LITH. & PUB. BY N. CURRIER.   152 NASSAU STREET N. Y.

THE AMERICAN PRIVATEER "GENERAL ARMSTRONG" CAPT. SAM. C. REID.

In the Harbor of Fayal (Azores) Oct: 26th 1814. Repulsing the attack of 14 boats containing 400 men from the British Ships 'Plantagenet 74'- 'Rota' 44. and 'Carnation' 18 Guns. The General Armstrong was 246 tons burthen Carried 6 Nine pounders and a Long Tom (42 pounder) amid ships and a crew of 90 men. The British loss was 120 killed

On September 26, 1814, a British squadron attacked the privateer brig *General Armstrong* of New York in the neutral port of Fayal in the Azores. Commanded by Norwich-born Captain Samuel Chester Reid, the Americans mounted a stubborn defense, as seen in this hand-colored lithograph published about 1830 by Nathaniel Currier. The attack actually took place at night, and Reid and his crew inflicted extensive casualties on their attackers before scuttling the *Armstrong* and escaping ashore. Reid's other patriotic contribution was a plan to redesign the American flag—with 13 stripes, and a star to represent each current state—that was adopted in the Flag Act of 1818.

(© Mystic Seaport Collection, Mystic, CT, #L1959.1164)

Constitution would finally make her escape from Boston on December 18, just a month after the USS *Hornet* slipped out of New London and ran up the Sound to New York. The *Hornet* would escape to sea that month too. The USS *President*, commanded by Stephen Decatur, would run the blockade of New York Harbor on January 13, 1815, only to be captured by a British squadron. By winter the US would again have some if its dangerous warships on the loose in the Atlantic.

War in the South

The spring of 1814 saw another major Native American defeat. Commanding Tennessee militia, a US Infantry regiment, and Cherokee, Choctaw, and Lower Creek natives, General Andrew "Old Hickory" Jackson attacked the Red Sticks, members of the Creek nation who had sided with Tecumseh and the British in an effort to resist American settlement on their lands in the Deep South. The Battle of Horseshoe Bend (in present-day Alabama), fought in late May of 1814, shattered the Red Stick force. More than 500 of the 1,000 Red Stick Creek warriors were killed, and about 200 took refuge with their brethren, the Seminoles, in Spanish Florida. The August 1814 Treaty of Fort Jackson punished not only the Creeks who had fought against Jackson, but also the Lower Creeks who had allied with the Americans and helped defeat their native kin. All told, the Creek people lost 23 million acres in central Alabama and southern Georgia to their Anglo-American neighbors.

"Old Hickory's" success against the native population notwithstanding, the British saw great vulnerability in the region. The third prong of the British 1814 campaign was aimed at the Mississippi Delta and the port of New Orleans. The invading force left Jamaica in November. Meanwhile, Jackson led his troops against Pensacola in early November and drove the British forces out of West Florida.

Mrs. Stewart's Situation

written by Andrew W. German

And as you engaged that Mrs. Stewart the wife of the British vice consul late resident at New London, with her family, shall be permitted to embark on board this Ship tomorrow morning, I am induced to wave the attempt of the total destruction of your town.

CAPTAIN SIR THOMAS MASTERMAN HARDY
TO THE MAGISTRATES OF STONINGTON,
AUGUST 10, 1814

—————————— •◆◆◆• ———————

Who was the woman who so influenced the Battle of Stonington?

Elizabeth Coles Stewart was born in England about 1778. Her father, John Coles, a British merchant of mixed success, took his family to America after the Revolutionary War. They were living in Boston when he decided to move on to New London in 1794. He purchased the large, and elegant Winthrop mansion north of town next to the town mill and quickly became one of New London's prominent merchants and social trendsetters. The family hosted memorably elaborate dinner parties, and Elizabeth grew up in the American version of English society.[1]

Probably through his West Indies trading connections, John Coles made contact with James Stewart, a personable Scotch/Irish merchant on the British island of Grenada. The connection was sealed in the marriage of the 34-year-old Stewart to Elizabeth Coles at New London in 1798. Stewart moved to New London and established his "Compting house" on Main Street. With his connections on Grenada and shares in a sugar plantation in Surinam, Stewart appeared to be thriving as a resident alien in America. Elizabeth managed their growing family: four girls and two boys by 1812.[2]

But her father's life was coming apart. John Coles and his wife reportedly separated, and in 1807 he defaulted on nearly $20,000 to New York merchants. The embargo closed New London's accustomed trade for 14 months, further damaging his business. When Boston merchants foreclosed on Coles's New London property in 1810, Stewart stepped in to buy it, establishing himself as his father-in-law's successor in New London. Now—although her father was disgraced—Elizabeth Stewart had one of the grandest homes in New London, complete with "a mahogany book case with a collection of choice books upon various subjects," fine tableware and tea sets, "elegant engravings" on the walls, and most remarkably, "an English made organ containing six stops, well ton'd and suitable for a church." The house remained an outpost of English civilization and good taste.[3]

In 1811, probably through the efforts of Thomas Barclay, the principal British consul to the United States, who lived in New York, Stewart was appointed the British vice consul at New London. His duties included attending to the needs of British captains or seamen who entered the port of New London, and representing the interests of British merchants in their local dealings. In 1812 he had a supply of trading licenses to issue or sell, which permitted passage to Spain or Portugal for the provisioning of British forces fighting Napoleon there, or to the neutral Swedish port of St. Bartholomew in the West Indies. St. Barth became a regular trading partner of New London after war was declared, and Stewart profited by selling licenses and acting as commission agent for the New London end of the trade. When Commodore Stephen Decatur's squadron arrived in New London, Stewart had $30,000 tied up in the business of several Swedish vessels in port. While hoping to get clearance for their departure, he knew they represented the end of his income as a British merchant and consul in wartime America. Desperate to expand his income and extend his duties in New London he asked Barclay, "Do you know the Swedish Consul General would he give one an appointment for this port or could the business be managed without knowing the Language or would the Spanish Minister appoint for his nation."[4]

Stewart was able to parlay his consular position into the role of agent for British prisoners of war who were brought to New London. The first arrivals were Captain John Carden and the crew of HMS *Macedonian*. The Stewarts took Carden into their home and housed the crew in their hay barn for a month. But Stewart was not good at accounting for his expenses or obtaining receipts for reimbursement, and he complained the fee he received "will not pay for the wine drank at the agents house." At the same time, with the British squadron right offshore, his frequent communication with Captain Sir Thomas Hardy over matters of British prisoners made him appear all too close to the blockaders, if not an outright conspirator in British plans against New London.[5]

By May 1813, Congress had voted to give British resident aliens in coastal communities six months to leave the country. Otherwise, they would be sent 40 miles inland to live under parole so they could not aid the British forces alongshore.

Without warning, Connecticut Marshal Robert Fairchild ordered Stewart to leave New London at the end of June. Stewart refused. Merchant Elisha Dennison and "9/10ths of the inhabitants," according to Stewart, petitioned Secretary of State James Monroe to permit Stewart to remain. Nevertheless, Fairchild had him forcibly removed to Stafford Springs, on the Massachusetts border, on July 1. Prone to believe in conspiracies against him, Stewart told Barclay: "I believe some false & Malicious information has been sent respecting my loading some Swedish vessels lately for Mr. Dickey & some houses in the West Indies, & some people at New London wishing the Commission themselves prevailed upon Decatur & other people to make the application to the Government to send me out of the way in addition to this[,] Parties beginning to run high & as a certain party [Federalist] were intimate with me, altho I never meddled with politics[,] that also operated,—I conceive it my duty while I remain in this country to see and strickly conform to the Laws and in no way shew any wish to oppose the Government."[6]

With a child on the way, Elizabeth remained in New London when her husband was banished. The authorities permitted Stewart to return for a few weeks to be with Elizabeth when she gave birth to a son in September. Stewart later claimed that he was soon turned over to the British and headed for Halifax aboard HMS *Atalante*, which was wrecked off Halifax early in November. Stewart and all on board were saved, and at Halifax he "tendered his services" to Admiral Sir John B. Warren, commander of British naval forces. Stewart traveled with Warren to Bermuda and talked his way into a position as victualer supplying provisions to the Royal Navy, though he did not have the resources to operate such a business. However, he believed he had the connections to supply an equally vital resource that was in short supply in Bermuda—hard cash—no doubt at benefit to himself. One aspect of the plan was to use his connections in the New London area to funnel money out, possibly aboard boats that would come out to the blockaders. Admiral Warren informed Captain Talbot of HMS *Victorious* about the plan in February, but a copy of his letter was captured, so Connecticut authorities were alert to this scheme.[7]

A second part of the plan was to syphon money by setting up shop aboard a vessel anchored in Gardiner's Bay. Smugglers were welcome to pay cash for scarce goods and take the risk of carrying them ashore. This was exactly the kind of scheme Stewart knew how to organize, and he engaged Thomas Barclay's son to manage the sales vessel. The operation seems to have begun in early August 1814, when the British squadron returned to local waters with Stewart on board. And apparently it worked. In the fall, a Stonington firm was discovered to have smuggled in $20,000 worth of goods from Stewart and Barclay's trading vessel.[8]

Some have speculated that Elizabeth Stewart acted as a secret agent for the British during her husband's absence. Long after the war, Captain Hardy and others endorsed the Stewarts' claim for a pension, noting the "very important and correct information of the enemy's movements" she provided. It is possible her home served as a stop for British agents who reportedly passed through New London, though there is no evidence that she managed an espionage ring or that New London authorities suspected her. A difficult pregnancy and the care of her infant son kept her busy at home during much of the time. However, she was known to have influence with the British officers, and on at least one occasion a loyal American took advantage of that. When two Mystic brothers were picked up by HMS *Maidstone*, "I procured their release, at the earnest entreaties of their mother, living at Mystic," Elizabeth Stewart wrote.[9]

On August 7, Admiral Henry Hotham sent a flag of truce in to New London requesting that Elizabeth Stewart and her children be sent out to the blockaders. General Thomas Cushing, the army commander at New London, forwarded the request to authorities in Washington. This bureaucratic delay made Elizabeth Stewart a bargaining chip during the attack on Stonington three days later, although the Stonington magistrates had no possibility of delivering her to Captain Hardy. The Madison administration did grant approval for her to leave, and on August 25 she and her children rejoined James after an eight-month separation. They settled in the Jerome house on Plum Island, where Stewart could supervise his operations, though he usually slept on shipboard to avoid kidnapping by American private armed boats.[10]

On September 21, Elizabeth persuaded her husband to stay ashore as he had suffered from exposure when his vessel stranded on Block Island two nights earlier. At midnight, persistent pounding on the door alarmed everyone in the Jerome house. Peeking out, the Stewarts saw six men. Frantically, Elizabeth hid her husband under a bed, with pillows and a chair to conceal him, then put their children in the bed. When Mr. Jerome opened the door, John Washington—a former British sailor who served as spokesman for Captain Burrows's private armed boat *Yankee* of Mystic—asked if any British officers were in the house. Recognizing Mrs. Stewart, he asked for her husband. She and Jerome tried to convince him that Stewart was on board HMS *Maidstone*. As the *Yankee* crew searched the house, Mrs. Stewart kept them from one room, "saying that there was nothing in it but her children, and that they were afraid." The crew barged in, and whenever they neared the bed, "around which the children were placed, the women and children would cry out." Their dramatics gave Stewart away. After they hauled him out, he argued, "it will be of no use, to take me, I know your government, they won't

This watercolor is titled *View of New London from the Home of James Stewart, British Consul at New London, dedicated to Mrs. Stewart by a poor shipwrecked Swiss sailor, 1815*. It appears to show Elizabeth Coles Stewart and two of her sons on the formal lawn, with part of New London's commercial waterfront in the distance. The Stewarts' home had been built at the head of Winthrop Cove, next to the New London Mill, by John S. Winthrop in 1754 and was purchased by Elizabeth Stewart's father in 1794. A bit of old English formality in New London, the house served as the British vice consulate from 1811 to 1832—except when the Stewarts were the center of controversy during the war. The house was razed for the Winthrop School in 1892 and is now a vacant lot next to the Old Town Mill.

(Lyman Allyn Art Museum, 1944.69)

detain me more than a week or two, and then they will let me go, and it will be an expense." He then offered them $100 to leave him, and Mrs. Stewart gave them what gold she had. Washington conferred with Captain Burrows at the boat, and returned to report that they could not take the money. "Mrs. Stewart said she would not take it [back] unless you will agree to leave Mr. Stewart." Washington vaguely agreed, "to pacify her," and she thanked him. "He then turned round and put his hand on Mr. Stewart's shoulder and told him to put on his cloaths and go with us, at which time Mrs. Stewart fainted."[11]

Always looking for the right price, Stewart raised his offer to $500 for his freedom, but Burrows refused. During the long night row back to Mystic, Stewart became his usual chatty self, expecting a brief confinement. But the authorities sent him on board the *United States*, where he was completely out of touch with any of his profit-making schemes. When Vice Admiral Alexander Cochrane heard of Stewart's capture, he threatened to seize every American he could and send them to England, and to resume attacks on the New England coast. After Stewart was paroled and lodged with his father-in-law, Cochrane relented. Still on Plum Island, Mrs. Stewart read the *Connecticut Gazette* report of her husband's capture and offered the last word: "I sincerely regret the American government are not fully possessed of all the particulars relating to this transaction; and which I have good reason to believe, they are not."[12]

After hostilities ended, the Stewarts returned to their New London home and apparently entertained Admiral Hotham when he visited New London at the beginning of March 1815. James resumed his position as British consul at a rate of £300 a year, and the Stewarts again played a popular role in town. In 1825 their daughter Isabella married the young whaling merchant (and future mayor) Noyes Billings, a match that brought her the prosperity and influence her parents and grandparents had aspired to. When the New London vice-consular position was abolished in 1832, James and Elizabeth Stewart sold their mansion to Billings and returned to the land of their birth to live on his half-pay pension and seek support from their government.[13]

So who was Elizabeth Coles Stewart? She was an Englishwoman who spent most of her life in America. She was the devoted daughter and wife of convivial, flawed men. She was also a busy mother who aspired to the trappings of British society. And even while a victim of war, the elusive Mrs. Stewart found her own ways to fight back.

The Hartford Convention as the Embodiment of Federalist New England

written by Dr. Matthew Warshauer

THE NOTORIOUS HARTFORD Convention, held in the latter days of the War of 1812, defines New England Federalism. This is true on two principal levels. First, the Convention represented a last-ditch effort on the part of the region to reclaim its waning political power. As part of the original thirteen colonies, and with Boston at the heart of the American Revolution, New England had enjoyed considerable influence over the burgeoning nation. That sway, however, was in decline almost immediately as the Southern and Western states continued to multiply in number, and in doing so expanded the ranks of the Republican Party. Federalists were largely cooped up in New England, with additional party devotees spread into parts of New York and the Middle-Atlantic states. The Louisiana Purchase was in many ways a death knell to the Federalists, promising further expansion of the nation, and hence a diminution of their own political power.

The second issue was the Federalists' outlook toward Great Britain and their overall opposition to the War of 1812, which had been initiated by James Madison's Republican administration. Disagreements over foreign policy stretched well back into George Washington's cabinet and largely subsumed his administration, dividing Secretary of the Treasury Alexander Hamilton (who favored the English mercantile system) and Secretary of State Thomas Jefferson (who wanted to avoid a rapid growth of manufacturing and maintained a belief in France as America's greatest ally). Not only did Federalists oppose the war, but as it continued they grew more and more concerned that New England's defense needs were not being met by the Republican administration in Washington.[1]

These factors are instrumental in understanding why 26 delegates from the five New England states (Massachusetts, Connecticut, Rhode Island, New Hampshire, and Vermont—the latter two sending delegates from particular counties rather than officially from the states) met from December 15, 1814, through January 5, 1815, at the State House in Hartford, Connecticut. The motivations of the Convention were debated before the delegates ever assembled. Beginning in November, the *Connecticut Courant* published a series of articles titled, "What is expected of the Convention at Hartford. What it can do and what it ought to do," announcing, "Our sovereignty is invaded. Our rights are trampled under foot. The Union which is an union of sovereignties has been violated by deserting some of them, while others have been unnecessarily defended, by drawing all the resources from some states which were endangered to defend others which were not. This is not one hundredth part of our wrongs and breaches of the Union."[2]

Given Federalist New England's rocky relationship with Republicans, its opposition to the war, and concerns over the region's defense, some theorized that the Convention's primary aim was secession from the Union and a separate peace and trade alliance with Great Britain. President Madison was so concerned with such an outcome that he sent Major Thomas S. Jesup to Hartford to report on the

The Hartford Convention or *LEAP NO LEAP.*

Immigrant Scottish artist William Charles (1776-1820) created this biting political cartoon titled *Hartford Convention or Leap no Leap* to mock the convention. It depicts Massachusetts radical Timothy Pickering praying at center, Massachusetts pulling Rhode Island and Connecticut toward the jump at left, and King George III of Great Britain encouraging them to jump into his arms. Charles's cartoon was published at Philadelphia by Samuel Kennedy in 1814.

(Library of Congress, Prints and Photographs Division)

proceedings.[3] Federalists insisted early on, and in the Convention's aftermath, that secession was not its aim. The Connecticut General Assembly appointed its delegates with the express instruction "to do nothing inconsistent with the states obligation to the union."[4] Calvin Goddard, a member of the General Assembly and delegate from Connecticut, wrote emphatically, "I am no rebel—have no scheme of severing the union. I should consider it an evil of no small magnitude if accomplished by a compact in the most peaceable way."[5]

The official "Report and Resolutions of the Hartford Convention," issued at its conclusion, revealed distinctly Federalist New England's concerns over the region's and the party's waning power since the nation's inception. Of the four resolutions and seven constitutional amendments proposed by the Convention, most dealt specifically with the balance of sectional power. More specifically, they advocated changing the congressional voting rules to favor the New England minority, insisting that no new states should be admitted without a two-thirds vote; no declarations of war should be made without the same (normal voting required only a simple majority on each); and the presidency should be limited to one term and that no person from the same state (i.e., Virginia) could be elected in succession. All of these, and other demands, represented the Federalists' attempt to reclaim their diminishing power.[6]

The Convention report also allayed concerns over potential secession and a separate alliance with England. Federalists made no mention of such radical notions; instead, they reflected on their concerns over New England's proper defense. Still, the final Convention resolution mixed these two issues with an implied threat, declaring that if the various proposals in the "Report" were not addressed and "peace should not be concluded, and the defence of these states should be neglected, as it has been since the commencement of the war, it will, in the opinion of this convention, be expedient for the legislatures of the several states to appoint delegates to another convention, to meet at Boston . . . with such powers and instructions as the exigency of a crisis so momentous may require."[7] Critics pondered what those powers and instructions might be.

With the miserable nature of the war—depredations on the New England coast, a failed ground campaign, and the August 1814 burning of the nation's capitol—Federalists undoubtedly felt confident in making such bold statements. But the unexpected announcement of the Treaty of Ghent (signed on Christmas Eve 1814) and the stunning victory at New Orleans by General Andrew Jackson (January 8, 1815) completely undid the Federalist power gambit and placed the final nail in the party's coffin. Republicans were able to spin the end of the war into a grand success for the nation and, in the warmth of a patriotic glow, cast Federalists as the ultimate traitors to the American cause. The party had done all it could to thwart the country's military, voting as a bloc in Congress over 90 percent of the time, first in opposition to the war's declaration, and then on measures that had to do with raising men and money or restricting trade with the enemy. New England governors refused to allow their militia troops to invade Canada, insisting that they were solely a defensive force, and Federalists in Hartford went so far as passing ordinances that restricted parades or the playing of martial music in order to dampen the spirit for recruitment.[8]

Such actions, crowned by the "secessionist" plot of the Hartford Convention, sank the already ailing Federalist Party. It never recovered, and to this day modern American political parties heed the sage historical lesson that one can oppose a war, but not the raising or funding of troops. The Hartford Convention has been forever tainted with the rumor of secession, though that was certainly not the initial Federalist goal. Rather, party members hoped to deal with two principal issues: their continuing decline of power in the early years of the new republic, and to voice their stern opposition to the war and the beleaguered position it had left the region in terms of defense. They succeeded in neither of these goals.

He then moved on to New Orleans, arriving shortly before the British expeditionary force arrived.

When the force of 8,000 British soldiers and sailors under Sir Alexander Cochrane and General Edward Pakenham, arrived on the Louisiana coast on December 12, their goal was a direct assault on the vital port of New Orleans, gateway to the Mississippi. Jackson had arrived in the unprotected city less than two weeks earlier and had been working tirelessly to mount a viable defense. His personal drive and skill in organizing and moving his troops, as well as the determined effort of Lieutenant Thomas ap Catesby Jones's gunboat flotilla on Lake Borgne east of New Orleans, contested the British advance. Moving slowly, the British forces were in position for their assault on January 8, 1815—10 days after the Treaty of Ghent ending the war was concluded by the negotiators. The 4,000 Americans, including some of the gunners from the Lafitte brothers' pirate band, held their earthworks between the Mississippi and a swamp on the Chalmette Plantation, less than eight miles south of the city. The elaborate British plans collapsed, so the battle was a forlorn hope advance by the British regulars against entrenched artillery and musketry. American losses, killed, wounded and missing were 71, including just 13 dead; the British total was 2,042, which included General Pakenham and 290 others killed.

The War Winds Down

The celebration of Jackson's victory was widespread in January of 1815, but that did not come in time to halt a challenge to the nation's viability as the world's only democratic republic. That challenge had gained momentum during the last year of the war, and was more from internal disputes than from that of the nation's declared enemy. Dissent from the states in the Northeast was the great threat, and Connecticut was a key player in that dissent. As noted earlier, Connecticut's representatives in Congress had not voted for the declaration of war, and throughout the conflict the state and its New England neighbors bridled against Washington's policies. In a number of cases, Connecticut Yankees moved from dissent and recalcitrance to open opposition against national policies.

There had been, for instance, Governors Griswold and Smith's refusal of the "unconstitutional" call to send Connecticut militiamen beyond state borders to support the war effort. President Madison noted that "if the authority . . . of the United States . . . can thus be frustrated . . . they are not one nation." Recruitment for the regular army was also hampered in Connecticut, and the influential clergymen of the state regularly railed against the central government. Connecticut was also unwilling to take on any of the cost of a war fomented by Republicans from other parts of the country. Eventually, the State Assembly voted 153 to 36 in December 1814 to send delegates to the Hartford Convention to identify strategies for mutual safety that were "not repugnant to our obligations as members of the Union."[3]

Five months before the blood-soaked Battle of New Orleans, envoys from the United States and Great Britain had first met to negotiate an end to the war. The American delegation, headed by John Quincy Adams, included such luminaries as Albert Gallatin and Henry Clay, among others. It took many months for the two nations to agree on the outcome. Since the defeat of Napoleon had ended the Royal Navy's need to impress sailors, the American negotiators gave up that major grievance even before negotiations began. But the Americans were surprised to find that, since they had declared war, there was a price to be paid. From the British perspective that price included the loss of Yankee fishing rights in Canadian waters, the loss of lands in present-day Minnesota and Maine, and a protected Native American region in the Old Northwest. With mixed military success in 1814, the

British fell back to *uti possidetis*, in which territory lost to enemy control is forfeited. The Americans held steady, and by October the British had abandoned the defense of Native American lands, and the negotiations moved toward settling on the situation as it was before the war (*status quo antebellum*). In fact, much larger issues being settled at the peace negotiations in Vienna, dealing with the future of Europe, and 1814's mixed success in the war against America, left the British weary of war and of negotiating. In the end, the belligerents resorted to *status quo antebellum*. All prisoners were to be repatriated, all occupied lands were to be abandoned, and so on. None of the causes of the war were addressed. The fighting simply was to stop . . . but not until both nation's had ratified the treaty.[4] News of the treaty arrived in New York on February 11, 1815, and the Senate approved the treaty five days later—and more than five weeks after the Battle of New Orleans.

Back in Connecticut, the Treaty of Ghent was met with great celebration, both ashore and in the British blockading squadron. "Capt. Bradley was on board the Superb, when the news of Peace was read to the crew," reported the *Connecticut Gazette*. "It was hailed in the most extravagant sailor-stile of joy; half of them threw their hats overboard. A double allowance of grog for the day added essentially to the happiness of the poor fellows, who have been perhaps for many a long year *"out adrift from the world."*—In the evening the officers between decks amused themselves with music and dancing."[5]

HMS *Narcissus* landed Captain Stephen Decatur in New London on Washington's Birthday, and he was mobbed by the happy residents. The next day he was the guest of honor at New London's peace ball in the courthouse, which included American military officers, about 15 British naval officers, and hundreds of residents. Describing the scene, the *Connecticut Gazette* reported: "But the most conspicuous and most interesting were the broad Ensigns of the U. States and G. Britain, which hung over the entrance of the front door, & extending side by side for 20 feet, then being twisted in the form of a wreath, dropped their points over the temporary orchestra. The reconciled friends embraced contributing to adorn & support each other."[6]

In Mystic, when the local men neglected to invite their wives to the celebration near Fort Rachel, Mrs. Holmes and Mrs. Haley took it upon themselves to fire off a cannon in their own private celebration. In Fairfield, festivities included roasting an ox on the green, as well as the traditional New England celebratory illumination, the burning of tar barrels. In this case, 18 were ignited. After several visits ashore by British officers—including one to order a gravestone for Midshipman Powers in Stonington—Admiral Hotham's squadron finally got underway on March 11, exchanging salutes with Fort Trumbull as it headed back to Great Britain. The embarrassments of the Hartford Convention aside, Connecticut was pleased to be free of war, and looked forward to a changed world.[7]

But naval actions continued on the high seas until news of peace traveled around the world. The *Constitution* had reached the coast of Africa, and on February 20 she defeated HMS *Cyane* and *Levant* there. More than a month later, on March 23, the *Hornet* would defeat HMS *Penguin* in the South Atlantic. The final naval action of the war would come more than four months after the treaty was approved, when the USS *Peacock* defeated the British East India Company brig *Nautilus* off Sumatra on the last day of June.

One might ask who were the winners, and who were the losers in the War of 1812. Madison's Republicans declared the United States the winner; it was the politically expedient thing to do. Looking back at the causes of the war would gain them nothing. Better to declare a glorious victory and look ahead to a more glorious future. The British people, on the other hand, quickly forgot about the sideshow that, for them, was the War of 1812. Their focus throughout had always been on the

U. S. Sloop of war Hornet, J. Biddle Esqr com^dr & H.M. Ship Cornwallis of 74 guns off the Cape of Good Hope — 1815.

Mariner William T. Skiddy joined the US Navy and received his midshipman's commission from President Madison. He reported to the sloop of war *Hornet* and served with that ship at sea after she escaped from New London late in 1814. While on board he employed his artistic talents to sketch and paint various scenes and events he experienced, including the *Hornet*'s narrow escape from a dangerous encounter with the 74-gun HMS *Cornwallis* off the Cape of Good Hope on April 27, 1815, more than two months after the US Senate approved the Treaty of Ghent, ending the war.

(© Mystic Seaport, William T. Skiddy Collection (Coll. 304), Mystic, CT)

Napoleonic threat, and his return to power at the beginning of March 1815 required a prompt military response that was only ended with his ultimate defeat at Waterloo on June 18, 1815. Today, few in the British Isles have any real knowledge of the 1812 war against the United States.

Ultimately, the greatest victors may have been the Canadians. They turned back invasion after invasion from the south, as they had during the American War for Independence. And, although the establishment of a unique Canadian identity would take time, the defense of their homeland did create heroes and myths that helped forge Canada's national character.

The great losers in the war—as they had been in the War for Independence—were the native peoples of the Northwest and the South. The victories by William Henry Harrison at Tippecanoe and the Thames in 1811 and 1813, and Andrew Jackson at Horseshoe Bend in 1814, undermined native self-determination in those regions.[8] The war also resulted in the acquisition of new land, particularly what had been West Florida, and the lands of native peoples in the Old Northwest and the South. The gobbling up of those Indian lands proved to be a precursor to the much greater expansion that a buoyant, "victorious" American citizenry embraced on the heels of the War of 1812, an expansion that came to be known as "manifest destiny."

The American declaration of victory ultimately may not have been as hollow as one would believe when considering the loss of blood and treasure for nothing more than the prewar status quo. With their northern border secured and demilitarized, and with Native power shattered, Americans swept into the great valley of the Mississippi. In little more than a decade the resultant economic and transportation revolution changed the face of the nation.

With the coming of peace in the seaports of Connecticut, and in ports all along the coast, change was taking place. Smaller ports, like Middletown and New Haven, joined others like Beverly in Massachusetts in losing their status as centers of international trade, becoming fishing towns or

The end of hostilities brought a renewal of maritime trade and related activity. However, Connecticut's foreign trade increasingly flowed through New York, and Connecticut shipyards expanded to supply New York's demand for new ships. Launched at Middletown, Connecticut, in 1816, the brig *American* was owned in New York and traded to the Mediterranean and South America. Marine artist Antoine Roux painted this watercolor at Marseilles, France, in 1820.
(©Mystic Seaport Collection, Mystic, CT, #1953.4558)

coastwise outports of the growing entrepots. New York most particularly saw its status as America's leading port of exchange grow over the next several decades. With peace, the transatlantic trade grew apace, and most of its energy was focused on New York. British dumping of goods in the city at war's end set up the long tradition of retailers making buying trips to New York. The city also became the center of finance, the American terminus of the revolutionary shipping concept of scheduled transatlantic packet ships after 1817, the nation's most important immigration center, and after 1825, the ultimate terminus for goods travelling east and west on the Erie Canal. America's maritime "Golden Age," between the War of 1812 and the Civil War, was in many ways New York's "Golden Age" as well, as it established itself as the nation's most important urban center.[9]

Some of the most vital players in that transition were, in fact Connecticut expatriates who had followed the money to New York when their own smaller ports faded under the stress of war. That exodus to the city began in the 1790s with the Griswolds of Old Lyme, who were followed by the Howlands of Norwich. The Griswolds and the Howlands became key American buyers in the lucrative China trade. Ultimately, Middletown native Samuel Russell became the leading American merchant in China through his Manhattan countinghouse. Other Connecticut natives who transplanted themselves and became successful New York entrepreneurs included Derby, Connecticut's Stephen Whitney, one of the city's first millionaires; Anson Phelps of Simsbury; Hartford's Elisha Peck; and his son-in-law William E. Dodge.[10]

There was also revolutionary change to the north and east of New York port, and much of it was sparked by the war. That revolution was industrial in nature, and its center was Rhode Island, Connecticut, and Massachusetts. Energy tapped at the fall lines of New England's many streams and rivers powered the region's industrial growth, particularly in textile production. The wartime absence of cheap British cottons in American markets encouraged investment in local production. Much of the capital that backed the industrial development came from the Yankee merchant houses that were forced away from the seafaring trades by uncertain markets, embargo, and war.

New England maritime merchants turned industrial capitalists are well represented by the Boston Associates, Francis Cabot Lowell, Nathan Appleton, and P.T. Jackson. These men had imported cotton goods from India, sometimes illegally, and when their trade was interdicted by the war they shifted their focus "from wharf to waterwheel" with their new textile factory in Waltham, Massachusetts. But their entrepreneur neighbors to the southwest in Rhode Island and eastern Connecticut had already established textile operations that helped spur the Boston Associates. Spreading out from Samuel Slater's mill near Providence (backed by maritime entrepreneur Moses Brown), elite investors and successful mechanics had carried the industrial seed from Rhode Island into eastern Connecticut's Coventry and Putnam on the Quinebaug River. Disruptions of foreign trade both before and during the war spurred the start of America's Industrial Revolution, and an important foundation of that revolution was the two dozen mills that sprang up in eastern Connecticut between 1809 and 1818. Industrialization spread across the state from Windham County, so that by 1818 there were also nine woolen mills in Hartford County, five in New Haven County, nine in Fairfield, eight up in Litchfield County, sixteen in New London County, four in Tolland, and five in Middlesex County. The spread of manufacturing influenced the demographics of the state in the years after the war as well. While small rural towns suffered the loss of population, burgeoning industrial communities experienced an increase of residents. In the census of 1820, only Rhode Island had a larger percentage of residents engaged in manufacturing. Sparked in large part by the interdiction of seaborne trade in the years before and during the War of 1812, Connecticut and Rhode Island led the nation in its shift in character from rural to urban.[11]

Maritime historians have often divided the early American story into the "Colonial Era," the "Heroic Era," and the "Golden Age." The Colonial Era ended with revolution in 1775, and the "Golden Age" of global reach and maritime expansion ran from 1815 to 1860. The middle period, the "Heroic Age," included all the years of conflict in the Atlantic World: the War for Independence, the age of neutral trade, and the War of 1812. These distinctive moments in the American maritime story are conflated because they all involved a fledgling United States struggling to get its footing in a broader world dominated by war, tension, and overwhelming foreign strength. The War of 1812 put that era to rest. With peace in Europe and in North America, the United States found itself ready to step on to the world stage, if not as an equal, then as the rising power in the western world.

The Glorious Tenth:
A Connecticut Town Remembers the War of 1812

written by James Boylan

AUGUST OF EACH YEAR marks the anniversary of the Battle of Stonington, the encounter during the War of 1812 when a substantial British naval squadron attacked a small coastal village, employing more than 160 cannon and firing more than fifty tons of shells, rockets, missiles, and cannonballs against only three cannons and a makeshift fort. On August 12, 1814, having failed to do whatever it was they intended to do, the British withdrew. The story of the battle was then trumpeted about the nation. Such an instance of success by a handful of amateur warriors against an overwhelming force of veteran professionals was a salve to national morale.

For its own part, Stonington declared victory. It has always unreservedly regarded the battle as a well-earned and glorious triumph, a miracle created by pluck and luck and worthy of commemoration. Yet, it was not seen as an occasion for gloating, but as an interval of instruction and thanksgiving. From the first anniversary, August 10—the second day of the battle—has served as the centerpiece of Stonington's own unique holiday, often celebrated with greater fervor than Independence Day itself.

The first celebration took place on August 10, 1815, a year after the battle, the first year of peace. Stonington's battle flag, the huge, shot-torn banner of 16 stars and 16 stripes, was raised at the 1814 fort, shown on old maps as a curved rampart facing to the south and west.[1]

A procession marched to the Congregational Church, listened to an address by the Reverend Ira Hart, and returned to the fort, where a prayer closed the day. On the evening of August 11, there was a "grand anniversary ball, the assembly being both numerous and brilliant." There was also a visit from the father of Midshipman Thomas Powers of the Royal Navy, who was killed a few days before the battle and buried with honors in Stonington.[2]

The tenth anniversary observance, in 1824, was even more ambitious. After the ceremonies and the oration, dinner was served at Major Paul Babcock's newly opened hotel on what later became Cannon Square. There were toasts. Stonington's famed seafarer, Captain Edmund Fanning, toasted "The Grasshopper Fort," a nickname for the battery. Samuel Copp toasted "American Eighteen-pounders"—the cannons that had defended the village. The toasts went on and on, covering the gamut of patriotic sentiments.[3]

A year later, church bells and the firing of one of the 18-pounders announced the day. Hundreds of spectators poured ashore from a chartered steamboat. There was a procession to church, a march to the battery and, finally, dinner at the hotel, with each toast followed by a salvo from the cannon. These observances set in place the custom that August 10 was to be a day of feasting and solemnity.[4]

If a speaker of years later is to be believed, Stonington almost lost the chief artifacts of the battle the next year. In 1826, the federal government evidently tried to haul away the 18-pounders (already 33 years old at the time of the battle) for scrap. They had been dragged to the dock when the people of the Borough realized what was happening, arrived in a swarm, took hold of the drag ropes, hauled them back, and saved them for posterity.[5]

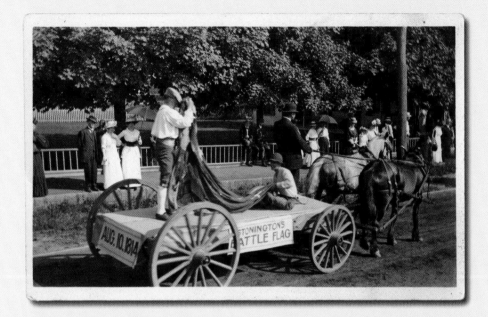

The fragile-looking relic held by the young men in this photographic postcard image is the Stonington battle flag of 1814, being carried on a wagon during the 1914 centennial celebration of the event. The boy standing and holding the flag is William K. Holmes Jr., the great-grandson of prominent Stonington defender Jeremiah Holmes.
(Courtesy of Stonington Historical Society, 2002.0613.402)

After the Civil War, new styles of observance appeared. Having turned prohibitionist, Stonington celebrated in 1872 with no toasts. David Frost, a preacher who had persuaded all but two lonely souls in the Borough to sign the pledge, led the parade. Still, there was food, served on the third floor of John F. Trumbull's factory, next to the old battery.[6]

The celebration in the national centennial year, 1876, was more expansive. It featured a 100-gun salute, bands, militia, and carriages containing "the Goddess of Liberty with thirteen young Ladies, representing the original thirteen States." There was an address in the Congregational churchyard and a poem on the battle, neither the first nor the last, by the Reverend Doctor Albert Gallatin Palmer. Then all adjourned to the sail loft on Water Street to eat. The *Stonington Mirror* was agog: "Indeed, in the wisdom of its conception, in the perfectness of its execution, in the wealth and variety of regalia, drapery and festoonings, in its well arranged march, in the military bearing of its marshals and officers and in the discipline so thoroughly enforced so generously and promptly accorded, in the abundant provisions of the tables and last though not least in the intellectual grade of speech and poem and hymn, we do not see how any improvement could have been made."[7]

The 1883 observance was notable for being one of the last in which a substantial number of those who had seen the battle of 1814 were in the procession. The most heroic figure, Captain Jeremiah Holmes, had died in 1872. Henry Denison, 90 years old, was listed as the sole participant present; six others were listed as eyewitnesses. Seven participants were said to be still living. The man said to be the last survivor, Captain Thomas Davison, died in 1894 at the age of 93, which meant that he would have served at the age of 13.[8]

Eventually, Stonington began to look toward the grandest celebration of all, the battle centennial of 1914. The organizing committee hired a pageant specialist, Virginia Tanner, Radcliffe '05, to assemble the main event. The celebration was spread over three days: Firemen's Day (Saturday), when five destroyers from the U.S. Navy arrived; Religious and Historic Day (Sunday); and Patriotic and Pageant Day (Monday).

Sunday featured church services and a long program of addresses, readings, and song before a huge crowd assembled in Wadawanuck Park.

Monday was climactic. At noon, a plaque provided by the Daughters of the War of 1812 was dedicated at the Atwood Company office building next to the site of the old fort; it was unveiled by Rosamond Spencer Holmes, great-great-granddaughter of Captain Holmes. (The plaque was stolen by parties unknown in the mid-1990s.) After the inevitable dinner at the Congregational Church parlors, the pageant parade, with 1,400 participants, got under way, with floats and marchers representing every epoch of Stonington history. According to the souvenir book published afterward, the parade "was generally hailed as a personal triumph for the resourceful and versatile director." Not content with directing, Virginia Tanner danced a sinuous solo in the dance program at Wequetequock Casino that evening.

The Monday crowd was estimated at 15-20,000, and the *Stonington Mirror* noted with satisfaction that the police had shooed away or locked up a number of notable crooks and pickpockets before they could ply their trade.[9]

Undeniably, the 1914 observance was the peak, the climax of Stonington's celebrations. Nothing that came after could match it. In 1934, a U.S. Navy destroyer paid a call and there was a banquet at Stonington Manor, a band concert, and fireworks. A year later, a big August 10 parade coincided with the Connecticut Tercentenary. Similarly, the observance of Stonington's tricentennial in 1949 was timed to coincide with the battle anniversary. The annual village fair, started three years later, was also placed on the Saturday nearest the anniversary, but has usually included no ceremonies relating to the battle. The last full-fledged observance came in 1964, on the 150th anniversary. It had a tree planting in Wadawanuck Square, a tour of houses and gardens, a horse show, a memorial service at Stonington Point, and fireworks on Sandy Point.

But no banquet.[10]

In 1990, the publication of James Tertius de Kay's book, *The Battle of Stonington*, revived interest. Not only did the work provide a broader understanding of the circumstances and the significance of the battle, but it gave the Stonington community a renewed sense that their town had been, for at least a moment, a focal point of national history. One symptom of renewed interest was the creation in 1997 of a musical, "The Battle of Stonington," based on the de Kay book, created by faculty members and presented by students at Stonington's Pine Point School.

But for the most part, observances since 1914 have been in an erratic decline. More than 35 years ago, the local historian Henry R. Palmer Jr. said that "the parades gradually dwindled to no more than a display of the Borough fire engines driving without bands or other fanfare silently around the Borough streets, and finally, to no parades or celebrations at all."[11] Competing observances appeared. For many years, the Blessing of the Fleet offered the feasting and dancing once associated with the battle anniversary, and a reinvigorated July 4 observance took over the patriotic fervor. Still, the Stonington Historical Society has tried, as the bicentennial of the battle approaches, to revive the August 10 observance, with mixed success, and the Borough of Stonington has started to make tentative plans for a community observance in August 2014.

But perhaps the diffidence that set in after 1914 is not all bad. One speaker at the centennial observance, Judge Gilbert Collins, proposed that a hundred years of celebrating the battle was enough—that thereafter an anniversary of peace be observed. And possibly that is what Stonington, by indirection and default, has done.

Legacies of the War of 1812 in Connecticut

written by Glenn S. Gordinier

IN CONNECTICUT there remain heroes, heroines, sites, and poetry that represent the War of 1812. Fairfield County's 1814 Powder House, the only such structure from the war in the state, enjoyed an award-winning restoration only a few years ago. Heavily built of local stone and covered with a cedar shingle roof, the building attests to the ongoing threat posed by the Royal Navy even along the western part of the Connecticut coast. The structure can be seen on the hill behind Fairfield's Tomlinson Middle School. The twenty-first century buzzes around the building, which sits halfway between the Old Post Road and I-95, but in the tense days of 1814, it was strategically located to supply coastal defense forts with gunpowder.

One can also visit the sites of a number of coastal batteries along the western reaches of the Connecticut coast. The location of the 1812 fort protecting Bridgeport Harbor can be seen today just behind the black Tongue Point Lighthouse. Militiamen fired on the privateer *Liverpool Packet* from this battery. The reconstructed Black Rock Fort, renamed Fort Nathan Hale, can be found adjacent to Coast Guard Station New Haven on the eastern shore of that harbor. A larger, Civil War-era fortification lies behind the earlier battery. The promontory a short distance away, then called Beacon Hill, was also the site of earthworks in what is now Fort Wooster Park.

Hartford is the site of the historic 1796 Old State House, then one of Connecticut's two capitol buildings. The classic structure was also the venue for the controversial Hartford Convention. The building, with its Senate Chamber where the secret meetings were held,

houses a fine historic exhibit and welcomes visitors.

Essex remains a classic New England village with its Main Street running, literally, into the Connecticut River. A visit to the lower reaches of the village still evokes that fearful night in April 1814 when British forces fired into and took control of that vital river port. The Connecticut River Museum, on the waterfront, contains artifacts of the attack.

British raiding parties entered almost every creek between Branford and Mystic during the war. In Clinton, a cannon commemorates the repulse of an assault. Fort Saybrook Monument Park in Old Saybrook marks the site of that historic defensive position at the mouth of the Connecticut River. In Niantic, the site of the Rope Ferry Bridge that burned during a British attack is near the current road and railroad bridges. Harkness Memorial State Park in Waterford occupies Goshen Point, off which a three-hour naval engagement occurred in 1814. Rogers's farm and a saltworks in the vicinity of Ocean Beach, New London, were repeatedly attacked by British cannon fire.

In New London, the site of James and Elizabeth Stewart's home is next to the Old Town Mill, which still stands beneath the southbound span of the I-95 Gold Star Memorial Bridge over the Thames River. On Bank Street, the doors of the customhouse—home to the New London Maritime Society—are made of wood from the USS *Constitution*. Across Bank Street, the Bulkeley House was home to Captain Charles Bulkeley, Revolutionary and War of 1812 privateer. At the head of State Street stands the 1784 courthouse

Although it is best known for the bloody engagement there in 1781, Fort Griswold became a heavily armed strategic defense against Royal Navy incursions once Commodore Decatur's squadron arrived in the Thames River in June 1813. As a Connecticut State Park, it is a monument to both wars.
(Courtesy of Mystic Seaport, Mystic, CT; Photographer: Dennis Murphy)

in which was held the grand peace ball in February 1815.

The environs of Forts Trumbull and Griswold are easily found and accessible on their respective sides of the Thames River. Fort Trumbull, close to sea level in New London is an evocative site but, except for an earlier magazine building, it is dominated by an imposing Civil War-era granite fortification. Fort Griswold's footprint atop Groton Bank on the eastern shore is similar to what militiaman Samuel Goodrich saw in 1813, but is more redolent of the bloody tragedy of September 1781.

The home of Mother Anna Warner Bailey was recently purchased by the City of Groton, which plans to renovate the historic structure. Bailey, who had seen with her own eyes the horror of the 1781 debacle at Fort Griswold, turned out in 1813 to contribute her petticoats when another attack on Groton Bank seemed imminent. As a resolute patriot, the aging tavern-keeper became a celebrity, and visitors—

including three American presidents—came to meet her through the years. The "Mother Bailey" House can be seen at the corner of Thames and Broad Streets in Groton, not far from Fort Griswold. This heroine's tombstone stands in the Starr Cemetery in Groton.

At Gales Ferry on the Groton side of the Thames River, north of today's US Submarine Base, one can walk the promontory that guarded the blockaded American warships in 1813. Fort Decatur held a commanding view of the waterway, and the Commodore's squadron was never challenged there at the foot of "Allyn's Mountain." An impressive remnant of the thwarted British threat is visible, however, in the form of a large ringbolt embedded in a riverside rock. The ring is said to have been the eastern anchor of a defensive chain that spanned the river.

Stonington Borough, with an 1814 monument at its point and the two cannon that actually defended the town now preserved on Cannon Square, cannot help but spark the visitor's imagination. Perhaps even more evocative are the several 215-pound "carcasses" fired by HMS *Terror* that can be found on granite posts here and there about the village. The Stonington Historical Society contains artifacts of the battle. Just half a mile up North Main Street one can also find the final resting place of the young British officer, Thomas Powers. His obelisk, purchased by his fellow officers in HMS *Superb* and now discolored by time, stands as a touching reminder of the pathos of war.

For a lighter sensibility one can consider a name associated with Connecticut—though not by birth or residence—Phillip Freneau. Well known in his day, Freneau had been a sailor and privateer during the War for Independence, but was more importantly a close friend of James Madison. The editor of the Democratic Party mouthpiece, *The National Gazette*, Freneau used his writing skills to help the Jeffersonian party in its assaults on Federalist policies. Also known as the "Poet of the American Revolution," Freneau penned the witty, and once popular poem, "The Battle of Stonington on the

Seaboard of Connecticut," celebrating the attack in 1814. One still chuckles when reading, in Freneau's words, how "They killed a goose, they killed a hen/Three hogs they wounded in a pen," and how "It cost the King ten thousand pounds/To have a dash at Stonington."

Largely ignored today, the War of 1812 deserves our attention and understanding. It helped change the face of Connecticut from a rural state that engaged in the Atlantic marketplace to a leading industrial center, whose maritime activities in its western reaches were dominated by New York port, as its eastern ports changed their focus to sealing, whaling, the fisheries, and shipbuilding. The War of 1812 also changed the character of the nation, a nation that found itself at war's end on the brink of rapid expansion, technological revolution, and a forthcoming status as a challenger in the global marketplace. The war deserves to be remembered for the suffering and sacrifice of its generation, as well as for its role as a catalyst that triggered a "Golden Age" in America's maturity and modernization.

Notes

Chapter One:
Profits, Tensions, and Neutral Trade

1. For the story of the 1781 attack on New London and Groton Heights, see Frances Manwaring Caulkins, *History of New London, Connecticut* (New London: author, 1852); Charles Allyn, *Narrative of Jonathan Rathbun: With the Narratives of Rufus Avery and Stephen Hempstead, Including the Narrative of Thomas Herttell* (1882; reprint, New York: Arno Press, 1999); Walter Powell, *Murder or Mayhem? Benedict Arnold's New London Connecticut Raid, 1781* (Gettysburg, PA: Thomas Publications, 2000). See also the unique pamphlet, *The Paragon-Jonathan Brooks of New London, Connecticut, Candidate for the Presidency* (New London, 1844), copy in G.W. Blunt White Library, Mystic Seaport.

2. Frances Manwaring Caulkins, *History of Norwich, Connecticut* (Norwich: Thomas Robinson, 1845), 468, 475-79.

3. See Edward G. Gray, *The Making of John Ledyard* (New Haven: Yale University Press, 2007).

3. See Robert G. Albion and Jennie Barnes Pope, *Sea Lanes in Wartime: The American Experience 1775-1945*, 2nd ed. (New York: Archon Books, 1968), 71-73.

4. Glenn S. Gordinier, "Versatility in Crisis: The Merchants of the New London Customs District Respond to the Embargo of 1807-1809" (PhD Diss., University of Connecticut, 2001), 56-58. The rock-bound pastures of eastern Connecticut simply could not sustain the large-scale production of wheat, corn, and other sewn crops. As a result, many of the vessels launched in the region had slight refinements in design and look. Although American neutral trading vessels were largely unexceptional in character, being of the "cod head-mackerel tail" design, a horse jockey might also be deeper amidships with a higher rail. This additional freeboard would help keep the large livestock, being transported on deck in makeshift stalls, from being swamped by boarding seas. This slight accommodation was an acknowledgement of the very hazardous nature of the horse-jockey trade.

5. Gaddis Smith, "The Agricultural Roots of Maritime History," *American Neptune* 44 (1984): 5-10.

6. For an examination of Connecticut politics during this era see Richard J. Purcell, *Connecticut in Transition, 1775-1818* (New York: Oxford University Press, 1918).

7. Adam Seybert, *Statistical Annals of the United States of America* (Philadelphia, 1818), 62, 317.

8. See Margaret E. Martin, *Merchants and Trade of the Connecticut River Valley, 1750-1820* (Northampton, MA: Smith College, 1939), 54-65; Gordinier, "Versatility in Crisis," 41, 96-100; Thomas R. Trowbridge, "A History of the Ancient Maritime Interests of New Haven," *Papers of the New Haven Colony Historical Society* 3 (1882): 146-50, 162-63.

9. "Abstract of Duties Payable in the District of New London on Merchandise, 1 January 1805-31 December 1807," Records of the New London Customs District, National Archives and Records Administration, Waltham, Massachusetts.

10. Donald R. Hickey, *Don't Give Up the Ship! Myths of the War of 1812* (Urbana and Chicago: University of Illinois Press, 2006), 21. Donald Hickey is the foremost authority in this country on the War of 1812. His work was relied upon heavily for this book. Reading his works is highly recommended.

11. Five years later, the Royal Navy returned the surviving American seamen (one had died of natural causes; the only real deserter had been hung). By way of example, see William M.P. Dunne and Frederick C. Leiner, "An 'Appearance of Menace': The Royal Navy's Incursion into New York Bay, September 1807," *The Log of Mystic Seaport* 44, no. 4 (Spring 1993): 86-92.

12. "Abstract of of the Tonnage of the Several Districts of the United States on the Last Day of December, 1807," *Commerce and Navigation 1789-1815* (Washington, DC: Gales and Seaton, 1832), 733-34;

Caulkins, *New London*, 649.

13. Glenn S. Gordinier, "Enterprise and Authority: Southeastern Connecticut Responds to the Jeffersonian Embargo," *Connecticut History* 49, no. 1 (Spring 2010): 33-55 It should be noted, however, that when adjustments are made for inflation and the nation's population growth, the profits from foreign trade were healthy, but not meteoric. That said, neutral trade was still seen as the key to a prosperous economy in the coffeehouses of America's seaports.

14. Ira Peskin, "Conspiratorial Anglophobia and the War of 1812," *The Journal of American History* 98, no. 3 (December 2011): 647-69.

SIDEBAR: **Connecticut Arms-Makers**

1. David R. Meyer, *Networked Machinists: High-Technology Industries in Antebellum America* (Baltimore: Johns Hopkins University Press, 2006), 84-89.

2. Harold L. Peterson, *The American Sword, 1775-1945* (New Hope, PA: Robert Halter, 1954), 23-24, 27, 29-30, 49-51.

Chapter Two:

War Comes to the Nation

1. Donald R. Hickey, *The War of 1812, A Forgotten Conflict* (Urbana and Chicago: University of Illinois Press, 1989), 41-42, 44-47.

2. Ibid., 73; Theodore Roosevelt, *The Naval War of 1812* (New York: G.P. Putnam & Sons, 1882), xx.

3. Hickey, *War of 1812*, 130

4. Thanks for this understanding goes to Joseph Greene, researcher and graduate of the Frank C. Munson Institute of American Maritime Studies.

5. After more than a century, and still in print, the classic work analyzing naval actions during the war remains Theodore Roosevelt's *Naval War of 1812*.

6. Hickey, *War of 1812*, 151-52.

7. Ibid., 152-53.

8. *Connecticut Gazette*, April 14, 1813.

9. Ibid., May 5, 26, 1813.

10. Stewart to Barclay, June 4, 1813, Box 6, Thomas Barclay Papers, MS 43, Patricia D. Klingenstein Library, New-York Historical Society.

11. Samuel Griswold Goodrich, *Recollections of a Lifetime, or Men and Things I Have Seen,* 2 vols. (New York: Miller, Orton and Mulligan, 1857), 1:474-75. He was also pleased to report that for his service he was given 160 acres of western land. "Say not that republics are ungrateful!" he proclaimed.

12. *Niles' Register*, July 3, 1813, 288; *Connecticut Gazette*, July 7, 1813.

13. Sylvanus Griswold, Journal Fragment, June 21-December 2, 1813, transcript copy in possession of the author, July 12, 1813; *Connecticut Gazette*, July 14, 21, 28, 1813.

14. Griswold Journal, November 28, 1813; *Connecticut Gazette*, December 1, 1813.

15. Frances Manwaring Caulkins, *History of Norwich* (Norwich: Thomas Robinson, 1845), 561; Cornelia P. Lathrop, *Black Rock Seaport of Old Fairfield, Connecticut, 1644-1870* (New Haven: Tuttle Morehouse & Taylor, 1930), 79.

SIDEBAR: **American Sailors in the War of 1812**

1. See for example William S. Dudley and Michael J. Crawford, eds., *The Naval War of 1812: A Documentary History,* 3 vols. (Washington, DC: Naval Historical Center, 1985-2002), 1:611.

2. Samuel Leech, *Thirty Years From Home, or, A Voice From the Main Deck: Being the Experience of Samuel Leech, who Was for Six Years in the British and American Navies; Was Captured in the British Frigate* Macedonian*; Afterwards Entered the American Navy, and Was Taken in the United States Brig* Syren, *by the British Ship* Medway (Boston: Tappan & Dennet, 1843), 40.

3. Ibid., 241.

4. "A table of the component parts of the ration allowed in the navy of the United States…" 1 January 1814. Box 33, Folder 9, Denison-Rodgers Family Papers, Coll. 356, in Henry Denison Papers, G.W. Blunt White Library, Mystic Seaport.

5. Although many Americans were wrongfully impressed, the British asserted that anyone born in the British Isles was forever a British citizen and subject to service in the Royal Navy. To protect American seamen from impressment the U.S. had begun in 1796 to issue protection certificates to American seamen, which included a physical description of the sailor and verification that he was an American citizen. The Royal Navy did not always honor these documents.

6. Leech, *Thirty Years From Home*, especially v-vi.

7. Ibid., 130-36.

8. "Casualties: U.S. Navy and Marine Corps," *Navy History and Heritage Command*, http://www.history.navy.mil/faqs, accessed October 27, 2011.

SIDEBAR: **Connecticut Privateers**

1. Connecticut privateersman George Coggeshall wrote the most comprehensive narrative of American privateers during the War of 1812, *History of the American Privateers, and Letters-of-Marque, During Our War with England in the Years 1812, '13 and '14* (New York: author, 1856). The most analytical treatment remains Jerome R. Garitee's *The Republic's Private Navy: The American Privateering Business as Practiced by Baltimore During the War of 1812* (Middletown: Wesleyan University Press for Mystic Seaport, 1977), which gives a brief history of privateering, 3-10.

2. See Garitee, *Republic's Private Navy*. Evidence of the process for Connecticut privateers is found in NARA Microcopy 588, War of 1812 Papers of the Department of State, page 39, and RG 21, USDC-CT, Case files, 1790-1915, Terms: Dec 1812-May 1813, Box 13, Charles Bulkley vs ship *Lord Keith*, Charles Bulkley vs Dry Goods, Charles Bulkley vs Sloop *Hero* Cargo, NARA, Waltham, Massachusetts.

3. Edgar S. Maclay, *A History of American Privateers* (New York: D. Appleton & Co., 1899), 411; the Connecticut Ship Database, 1789-1939, indicates the *Actress* was built at Guilford in 1811. Commission 61, Benjamin Pendleton, July 22, 1812, Schooner *Lewis*, NARA Microcopy 588, War of 1812 Papers of the Department of State, page 39; the Connecticut Ship Database, 1789-1939, indicates the *Lewis* had been built in Massachusetts in 1801. The *Lewis* captured one ship and armed it, but was captured by *Hope Tender*, August 13, 1812, and sent into Halifax.

4. Commission 62, Oliver Champlin, September 26, 1812, Schooner *Joel Barlow*, NARA Microcopy 588, War of 1812 Papers of the Department of State, page 39; *Connecticut Gazette*, October 14, December 9, 1813, January 13, 1814.

5. Commission 63, Charles Bulkeley, November 2, 1812, Schooner *Mars*, NARA Microcopy 588, War of 1812 Papers of the Department of State, page 39; Journal of Private Armed Schooner *Mars*, November 1812-March 1813, MSS 828, Box 12, Folder 8, Rhode Island Historical Society; Caroline Fraser Zinsser,

Vine Utley: The Remarkable Country Doctor of Lyme, Connecticut (Niantic: East Lyme Public Library, 2010). The *Mars* was probably about 120 feet on deck, with a rig extending nearly 200 feet from jibboom to end of her spanker boom. She may have been built by Amasa Miller of New London, who built a similar-sized privateer in 1814, *Connecticut Gazette*, February 23, 1814.

6. *Connecticut Gazette*, May 5, 1813.

7. *Connecticut Gazette*, April 14, 21, 1813; Rev. Frederic Denison, ""Capture of the Sloop *Fox*," *Mystic Pioneer*, May 21, 1859; Commission 64, Ambrose Burrows, April 13, 1813, Sloop *Hero*, NARA Microcopy 588, War of 1812 Papers of the Department of State, page 39; Ambrose Burrows went back to sea in December 1813 as sailing master of the Baltimore privateer *Rolla*, but she was captured by HMS *Loire* before she had gotten off soundings, and Burrows spent the rest of the war in captivity, Rev. Frederic Denison," *Mystic Pioneer*, September 24, 1859.

8. *Connecticut Gazette*, January 12, 1814; the other boats were named *True Blooded Yankee, Defiance, Lively, Argo, Viper, Ramillies*, and *Yankee*, NARA Microcopy 588, War of 1812 Papers of the Department of State, page 39; *Connecticut Gazette*, March 2, August 24, October 5, 26, November 9, December 7, 1814; Rev. Frederic Denison, "The Barge Yankee," *Mystic Pioneer*, June 4, 1859.

9. *Connecticut Gazette*, December 16, 1812, January 6, 13, 27 1813; see also http://www.1812privateers.org/United% 20States/htm, accessed January 2012; Coggeshall, *History of American Privateers*, 220-21, 99, 105-09; James Terry White, *National Cyclopaedia of American Biography* 8 (New York: James T. White, 1898), 97-98; George Coggeshall, *Voyages to Various Parts of the World, Made Between the Years 1799 and 1844* (New York: D. Appleton, 1851), 33-41, 49-55, 76-109; Nathan Gillette Pond, "The Ponds of Milford," *The Connecticut Magazine* 10, no. 1 (January-March 1906): 172; Shaler to Agents, January 1, 1814, John Brannan, *Official Letters of the Military and Naval Officers of the United States During the War With Great Britain* (Washington, DC: Way & Gideon, 1823), 293-94; Captain Shaler was lost at sea aboard the *Governor Tompkins* in 1814.

10. Garitee, *Republic's Private Navy*; John A. Tures, "A Word of 'Captain Caution': Myths About Privateers in the War of 1812," *The War of 1812 Magazine* 14 (October 2010).

11. RG 21, USDC-CT, Case files, 1790-1915, Terms: Dec 1812-May 1813, Box 13, Charles Bulkley vs ship

Lord Keith, Charles Bulkley vs Dry Goods, Charles Bulkley vs Sloop *Hero* Cargo, NARA, Waltham, Massachusetts. The *Lord Keith* sold for $2706.95, dry goods from the *Richard* sold for $4739.76, fruit from the *Hero* sold for $3180.45 (duty $439.81), and the *Hero* sold for $5366.63 Total $15,993.79. Her other prize landed in Charleston, South Carolina, and record of her sale has not been found, but probably totaled about $10,000.

12. Garitee, *Republic's Private Navy*; Tures, "A Word of 'Captain Caution.'"

SIDEBAR: **Connecticut's Militia**

1. Orderly Book, 1803-1813 [Third Brigade], Connecticut Militia and Military District, Connecticut Historical Society (hereafter cited as CHS).

2. "An Act for the better regulating of the Militia of this Colony, and putting it in a more ready Posture for the Defense of the same," Charles J. Hoadly, ed., *Public Records of the Colony of Connecticut, Records from Oct. 1735-Oct. 1743*, vol. 8 (Hartford: Case, Lockwood & Brainard, 1874), 277-81.

3. "An Act in addition to and alteration of the statute entitled 'An Act for the forming and conducting the military force of the state,'" vol. 1, doc. 59, Connecticut Archives, War of 1812, [microform] Connecticut State Library (hereafter cited as CSL).

4. See various documents, Connecticut Archives, Militia, Third Series, October 1728-May 1820, [microform] CSL.

5. Third Regiment Muster Rolls, 1814, Box 1, Folders 7, 8, War of 1812, Records of Connecticut Militia, CHS.

6. "Our Militia," *Hartford Courant*, July 28, 1812.

7. "General Orders…uniform dress for the militia…," February 17, 1812, vol. 1, doc. 24, Connecticut Archives, War of 1812, [microform] CSL.

8. Third Regiment Receipt Rolls, 1814, Box 1, Folder 5, War of 1812, Records of Connecticut Militia, CHS.

9. "An Act in addition to and alteration of the statute entitled 'An Act for the forming and conducting the military force of the state,'" vol. 3, doc. 36, Connecticut Archives, War of 1812, [microform] CSL.

10. See Thomas Shaw Perkins Letter Book, vol. 2, 1813-1814, New London County Historical Society (hereafter cited as NLCHS). Perkins was aide-de-camp to Major General William Williams of the state militia.

11. See for example Thomas Shaw Perkins Letter

Book, vol. 1, 1813, NLCHS; vol. 2, doc. 74, Connecticut Archives, War of 1812, [microform] CSL.

12. See Thomas Shaw Perkins Letter Book, vol. 1, 1813, NLCHS.

13. Orderly Book, 1803-1813 [Third Brigade]. Connecticut militia and Military District, CHS.

14. Frances Manwaring Caulkins, "An 1828 Excursion from Norwich to Stonington," quoted in *New London County Historical Society Newsletter* (July-August 2009).

15. Gov. Joseph Cotton Smith, "on the restoration of peace…," May 1815, vol. 1, doc. 20, Connecticut Archives, War of 1812, [microform] CSL.

Chapter Three:
The Battle of Long Island Sound

1. This chapter is adapted from James Tertius de Kay, *The Battle of Stonington: Torpedoes, Submarines, and Rockets in the War of 1812* (Annapolis: Naval Institute Press, 1990).

2. *Connecticut Gazette*, June 30, July 21, 1813; James Know Laughton, "Sir Thomas Masterman Hardy," in *Dictionary of National Biography*, Vol. 8 (London: Oxford University Press, 1937-38), 1243-45; John Scudder claimed that atrocities in the West, where he had relatives, led to his sponsorship of the *Eagle*, *Niles' Register*, July 24, 1813, 344; Captain Riker later regretted the *Eagle* affair, "as several lives were lost without any use," *Connecticut Gazette*, July 7, 1813.

3. Rev. Frederic Denison later wrote: "various torpedo plots were laid. One from New London resulted in the death of the operator, Mr. Halsey," in "The Torpedo Adventures," *Mystic Pioneer*, June 18, 1859; Colt Papers, Box 9, Connecticut Historical Society. Colt misunderstood Halsey's middle name and spelled it Clowden. He was Silas Plowden Halsey, born in 1787 to Preston lawyer and militia officer Jeremiah Halsey and his wife Esther Park. Colt indicates that Halsey's bomb was made by New London metalworker John Sizer. Colt gives the date of Halsey's death "in New London Harbor in an effort to blow up a British 74" as 1814, though 1813 is more likely. To this day there is speculation that connects Halsey with David Bushnell, a native of nearby Saybrook, Connecticut, who had in fact designed and built a working submarine during the Revolution. That submersible, named the *Turtle*, was actually used in New York Harbor in 1776 in an unsuccessful attempt to sink Admiral Howe's flagship. Like Bushnell's, Halsey's

submarine included a water cock to let in water to submerge, a hand-operated force pump to evacuate the water, a hand-operated propeller crank that also served as an auger to attach a torpedo to an enemy ship's hull, a "conning tower" around the operator's head, and an air tube. However, Bushnell had gone to France and then vanished in 1787, and was living in Georgia under the name David Bush at the time of the war, see "David Bushnell (1740-1826)," *New Georgia Encyclopedia*, http://www.georgiaencyclopedia.org, accessed March 2012.

4. *Niles' Register*, August 7, 1813, 375; "It is true, that Diving Bells, Torpedoes, and "machines infernal" are literally *kept in soak* for the enemy, should they dare to come into our harbor" reported the *Connecticut Gazette*. "Since the attempt of the renowned *Halsey* of Preston, in a Torpedoe, the British ships have taken new ground for anchorage; & for some time before tripped their anchors every few hours. The commodore has frankly confessed that the apprehensions of some yankee trick has given him great anxiety. He knew of the Halsey Torpedoe, and mentioned the names of persons whom he said were the proprietors. He confesses that the torpedoes are among the acknowledged weapons of national warfare; altho' personally opposed to them," *Connecticut Gazette*, July 21, 1813; John Gore, *Nelson's Hardy and His Wife* (London: John Murray, 1935).

5. *Connecticut Gazette*, August 4, September 15, 1813; William S. Dudley, ed., *The Naval War of 1812: a Documentary History*, vol. 2, 1813 (Washington, DC: Naval Historical Center, 1992).

6. *Connecticut Gazette*, January 26, 1814.

7. Rev. Frederic Denison, "The Torpedo Adventures," *Mystic Pioneer*, June 18, 1859; Holmes had conferred with Decatur about the attack, and actually set out from the *United States* in the Thames River, not from Mystic. His boat was owned and fitted out by Mott & Williams of New York. After the failed attack on HMS *La Hogue*, Holmes's *Young Hornet* made an expedition east to Vineyard Sound, hoping to use the last torpedo on a British frigate in those waters, but without success.

8. De Kay, *Battle of Stonington*, 128-31; *Niles' Register*, July 9, 1814; document in Public Records Office, London, Crown Copyright ADM 1/4369; *Connecticut Gazette*, June 29, July 6, 1814. Berrien's *Turtle* had actually first come down the Sound in August 1813 but was chased for nine miles by British barges and went back to New York, *Connecticut Gazette*, September 1, 1813. Captain Hardy believed the

boat was associated with Thomas Welling of Long Island and Joshua Penny, who had guided the expedition to kidnap Hardy, for which Hardy seized Penny, *Connecticut Gazette*, September 15, 1813.

9. During the war, the most common Congreve rocket was a 32-pounder with a 15-foot guide pole. The rockets were similar to artillery shells: some explosive, some filled with small projectiles, and some filled with incendiary material to set fires. The rockets had a range of up to two miles, but little accuracy. At sea, the rockets could be fired on shipboard—the first vessel outfitted as a rocket ship, HMS *Erebus*, would serve in the Chesapeake—or from ships' barges fitted with launching racks.

SIDEBAR: **The Blue Lights**

1. *Connecticut Gazette*, October 27, November 3, December 1, 8, 15, 22, 1813, January 12, 1814.

2. *Connecticut Gazette*, January 12, 1814.

3. *Connecticut Gazette*, January 12, February 2, 1814.

4. Robert Fairchild to James Madison, January 3, 1814, James Madison Papers, Box 2, Folder 4, New York Public Library; *Connecticut Gazette*, January 12, 1814; the perpetrators of the blue lights were never identified.

5. Samuel Griswold Goodrich, *Recollections of a Lifetime, or Men and Things I Have Seen*, 2 vols. (New York: Miller, Orton and Mulligan, 1857), 1: 484-86.

6. Divisions within New London are made clear by editor Samuel Green's remark: "Some petulant scribblers of this place, continue through the Boston prints to trouble the public and disturb good neighborhood, with their whim-whams about the blue lights. These writers are another sect of "New-Lights," fancying themselves gifted with an intuitive kind of wisdom, which enables them to come directly at truth without the deductions of reason," *Connecticut Gazette*, January 26, 1814.

SIDEBAR: **The Burning of the Fleet**

1. Donald Malcarne, *Houses of Essex* (Essex: Ivoryton Library Association, 2004), 26.

2. Richard Coote to Captain Capel in command of the British squadron off New London the Admiralty, April 9, 1814. British Admiralty Dispatch Papers, 1/506, 274-80; Coote's report is included in "The Essex Raid: Captain Richard Coote and the *Connecticut Gazette*," in W.D. Wetherell, *This American*

River: Five Centuries of Writing About the Connecticut (Hanover: University Press of New England, 2002), 56-59; Richard Coote's naval rank was commander, but he is called captain by his superiors and was promoted to post captain after this raid; the men came from HMS *La Hogue, Endymion, Maidstone*, and *Borer*, and they traveled in three barges (carrying the Marines), two smaller gigs, and a sailing pinnace. The privateer advertised in New York was Richard Hayden's 318-ton schooner *Black Prince*. There has also been speculation that the raid was retaliation for repeated torpedo attacks on the blockading ships.

3. Coote to Capel, 274-80.

4. Russell F. Anderson, "The British Raid on Essex, April 8, 1814" (unpublished manuscript, Essex Historical Society, 1981), 2. Speculation that an exchange of signs by Free Masons on both sides dissuaded the British from burning the town has never been confirmed.

5. This accounting comes from the detailed list of vessels reported to the Admiralty by Captain Coote and does not include the two privateer hulls the British tried to take downriver, which bring the total to 27.

6. *Connecticut Gazette*, April 13, 1814; reprinted in "The Essex Raid: Captain Richard Coote and the *Connecticut Gazette*," in W.D. Wetherell, *This American River*, 59-61.

7. Coote to Capel, 274-80. Coote suggests that, before they embarked from Pettipauge, the inhabitants offered the sailors rum to delay them through drunkenness, but they maintained their discipline and declined the temptation; the privateer brig *Young Anaconda* was a potential successor to the Middletown privateer brig *Anaconda*, which was captured by the British in 1813.

8. The *Connecticut Gazette*, April 13, 1814, reports that the privateer schooner in which the British had stowed the cordage and sails, and then cut the masts before burning, was saved. This was certainly the schooner *Eagle*, which was not listed among the vessels destroyed.

9. Alexander Cochrane to John Wilson Croker, May 10, 1814, British Admiralty Dispatch Papers, ADM 1/506, 269-71; The *Connecticut Gazette*, April 13, 1814, speculated that the guide was an American who "had frequently been there with fish for sale."

10. Coote to Capel, 274-80.

11. *Connecticut Gazette*, April 13, 1814. The paper indicates that a brig and a schooner under construction in North Cove and set afire by the British, were saved by the residents; Coote's estimate of six privateers mounting 130 guns is a gross exaggeration based on counting gunports, not guns.

Chapter Four:
"The Attack Upon Stonington Point in 1814"

1. Manuscript in Box 2, Folder labeled F.M.C. Historical Manuscripts, F.M. Caulkins, Historical, New London County Historical Society.

SIDEBAR: **HMS *Terror***

1. Chris Ware, *The Bomb Vessel* (Annapolis: Naval Institute Press, 1994), 9, 64-67, 88, 91. For defense, the *Terror* also mounted eight 24-pound carronades.

2. *Connecticut Gazette*, August 17, 24, 1814. British bomb vessels were also used at Fort Washington, Maryland, August 27, 1814; Fort McHenry, September 13-14, 1814; and Fort St. Philip, Louisiana, January 9-19, 1815.

SIDEBAR: **Jeremiah Holmes and the Battle of Stonington**

1. James Tertius de Kay, *The Battle of Stonington* (Annapolis: Naval Institute Press, 1990), 16-17.

2. Rev. Frederic Denison, "Narrative of Capt. Jeremiah Holmes of Mystic Bridge, Connecticut, 1859," G.W. Blunt White Library, Mystic Seaport. A photocopy is available at http://library.mysticseaport.org/initiative/PageImage.cfm/PageNum=1&BibID=25275. The narrative was published as "The Voyages of an Old Sea Captain," *Historical Footnotes* 5, no. 1 (November 1967): 14-15; 5, no. 2 (March 1968): 10-15; and 5, no 4 (October 1968): 6-11.

3. See Rev. Frederic Denison, "Defense of the Sloop *Victory*," *Mystic Pioneer*, May 28, 1859, "The Torpedo Adventures," *Mystic Pioneer*, June 18, 1859, and "Seizure of Vessels," *Mystic Pioneer*, August 6, 1859.

4. De Kay, *Battle of Stonington*, 102-06, 110.

5. Richard K. Murdoch, "British Documents on the Stonington Raid, August 1814," *Connecticut Historical Society Bulletin*, 37 (July 1972): 73; Rev. Frederic Denison, "The Bombardment of Stonington," *Mystic Pioneer*, July 2, 1859.

SIDEBAR: **The Reverend as Barometer**

1. Jon Latimer, *1812: War with America* (Cambridge: Belknap Press of Harvard University Press, 2007), 34 (votes in House and Senate); Gary Wills, *James Madison* (New York: Henry Holt, 2002), 96 (gives the votes as 78-45 and 18-13); *The Public Statutes at Large of the United States of America* (Boston: Charles C. Little and James Brown, 1845), 2: 786 (joint resolution); James D. Richardson, *A Compilation of the Messages and Papers of the Presidents* (Washington, DC: Bureau of National Literature, 1897), 2: 498 (Madison's July 9 proclamation).

2. The hand-written sermon, in the Woolworth Library of the Stonington Historical Society, is not signed, but the handwriting is that of Ira Hart. Portions of the sermon appeared in Meredith Mason Brown, "Why Do Ye Wrong One to Another? Stonington at the Start of the War of 1812," *Historical Footnotes* (August 2010): 4-6.

3. Russell F. Weigley, *History of the United States Army* (New York: Macmillan, 1967), 125. The governor of Massachusetts also refused to call up that state's militia for the American campaign to take Montreal, Wills, *Madison*, 103.

4. James Tertius de Kay, *Battle of Stonington* (Annapolis: Naval Institute Press, 1990), 110-23 (Cochrane's order and the British taking of Eastport, Maine), 134-35 (killing and burial of Powers); Richard Anson Wheeler, *History of the Town of Stonington* (New London: Press of The Day Publishing Co., 1900), 67 (killing and burial of Powers).

5. Madison to Wilson Cary Nicholas, November 16, 1814, *The Writings of James Madison*, vol. 8, 1808-1819 (New York: G.P. Putnam's, 1908), 319.

6. De Kay, *Battle of Stonington*, 146-83; Wheeler, *History of Stonington*, 74 (letter from Amos Palmer to William H. Crawford, Secretary of War, August 21, 1815), 70 and 417 (Hart as chaplain of Col. Randall's regiment at the Battle of Stonington), and 67-68 (Hart with Powers's father at Powers's grave).

SIDEBAR: **British Barges and Yankee Tricks**

1. *Connecticut Gazette*, September 22, 1813, gives a description of a British barge that absconded from HMS *Acasta* and arrived in Stonington, *Connecticut Gazette*, May 4, 11, 25, 1814. Regarding the English woman on the packet *Mary*, the *Gazette* reported" "The English woman said she was the wife of a Doctor, who was at New-London, and going to Bermuda in a cartel [prisoner exchange vessel]. A few nights previous an Englishman of this description and a Lieut., who put up at Brown's Coffee-House, stole a boat belonging to a poor citizen and went off to the blockading squadron."

2. Rev. Frederic Denison, "Attempted Burning of Mystic," *Mystic Pioneer*, June 25, 1859; Rev. Frederic Denison "The Ruse at Long Point," *Mystic Pioneer*, July 16, 1859; soon after, the militia and boatmen tried to lure another barge to Groton Long Point, but the barge halted off the beach and exchanged shots with the militia before retiring, Rev. Frederic Denison, "Second Adventure at Long Point," *Mystic Pioneer*, August 6, 1859.

SIDEBAR: **The Battle of Goshen Point**

1. Spencer C. Tucker, *The Jeffersonian Gunboat Navy* (Columbia: University of South Carolina Press, 1993), 16-17, 65, 70.

2. *Niles' Register*, April 2, 1814, 7; the assignments in 1814 were: Portsmouth 6, Newburyport 2, Boston 2, New Bedford 2, Newport 7, New London 2, New York 38, Delaware Bay 19, Baltimore 1, Potomac River 3, Norfolk 23, North Carolina 6, Charleston 2, Georgia 5, New Orleans 6; *Connecticut Gazette*, January 19, 1814; Gunboats 89-92 were built at Norwich and Westerly in 1808 and were armed with single 24-pounders, Tucker, *Jeffersonian Gunboat Navy*, 59, 114, 193.

3. Rocellus S. Guernsey, *New York and Vicinity During the War of 1812-'15* (New York: Charles L. Woodward, 1889, 1895), 1:122, 2:41-42; Tucker, *Jeffersonian Gunboat Navy*, 116-17.

4. *Niles' Register*, August 14, 1813.

5. Sylvanus Griswold, Journal, June 21–December 2, 1813, transcript copy in possession of the author. August 4, 1814.

6. *Niles' Register*, June 4, 1814, 225; June 11, 1814, 248.

7. *Connecticut Gazette*, June 1 1814.

8. *Niles' Register*, June 4, 1814, 225.

9. Tucker, *Jeffersonian Gunboat Navy*, 162-70.

Chapter Five:
An End to the War

1. Ernest J. King, *The Coast Guard Under Sail: The U.S. Revenue Cutter Service 1789-1865* (Annapolis: Naval Institute Press, 1989), 59.

2. Melvin H. Jackson, "The Defense of the Revenue

Cutter *Eagle*; Or a New View on Negro Head," (unpublished typescript, Division of Naval History, Smithsonian Institution, n.d.), 1-18, http://www.uscg.mil/history/articles/1812EagleJacksonMelvin002.pdf, accessed January 2012.

3. Albert E. Van Dusen, *Connecticut* (New York: Random House, 1961); Richard J. Purcell, *Connecticut in Transition, 1775-1818* (New York: Oxford University Press, 1918), 289-90, 293.

4. Donald R. Hickey, *Don't Give Up the Ship! Myths of the War of 1812* (Urbana and Chicago: University of Illinois Press, 2006), 278, 295-96.

5. *Connecticut Gazette*, February 22, 1815.

6. Ibid., February 22, March 1, 1815.

7. Rev. Frederic Denison, "Celebration of Peace," *Mystic Pioneer*, August 20, 1859; Cornelia P. Lathrop, *Black Rock Seaport of Old Fairfield Connecticut 1644-1870* (New Haven: Tuttle Morehouse & Taylor, 1930), 81; *Connecticut Gazette*, March 8, 15, 1815.

8. For an informative discussion of this topic see Hickey, *Don't Give Up the Ship!*, 296-305.

9. The classic study of the development of New York as America's leading entrepot remains Robert G. Albion's *The Rise of New York Port, 1815-1860* (1939; Boston: Northeastern University Press, 1984).

10. Robert G. Albion et al, *New England and the Sea* (Middletown, Connecticut: Wesleyan University Press, 1972), 105; Albion, *Rise of New York Port,* 246-49; Cornelia P. Lathrop, *Black Rock Seaport of Old Fairfield Connecticut 1644-1870* (New Haven: Tuttle Morehouse & Taylor, 1930), 81; David R. Meyer, *The Roots of American Industrialization* (Baltimore: Johns Hopkins University Press, 2003),100-05; Van Dusen, *Connecticut*, 187.

SIDEBAR: **Mrs. Stewart's Situation**

1. R.B. Wall, "New Londoners Recall When Mill Wheel Turned Daily," *New London Day*, in R.B. Wall Scrapbooks, 539; "Aunt Liddy's Diary," *New London Day*, January 9, 1911, R.B. Wall Scrapbooks, 599, New London County Historical Society; Coles may be the John Coles of London, formerly of New York, who was listed as bankrupt in the *London Magazine*, 1783, 279.

2. New London Vital Records; Stewart to Barclay, July 3, 1813, Box 6, Thomas Barclay Papers, MS 43, Patricia D. Klingenstein Library, New-York Historical Society (hereafter cited as N-YHS); Wall, "New Londoners Recall When Mill Wheel Turned Daily,"

R.B. Wall Scrapbooks, 539, Wall locates Stewart's New London office on Main Street (now State Street) opposite Richards Street; it is possible Stewart was related to the John Stewart who purchased Grenada properties about 1790 and also owned Surinam plantations, http://www.historyofparliamentonline.org/volume/1790-1820/member/stewart-john-ii-1755-1826, accessed February 2012.

3. David Ludlow et al. v. John Coles, New London County Court Files, June 1807, Box 272, Folder 8, no. 19, Connecticut State Library; Wall, "New Londoners Recall When Mill Wheel Turned Daily," R.B. Wall Scrapbooks, 539; "Aunt Liddy's Diary," R.B. Wall Scrapbooks, 599, suggests that Mrs. Coles tried to drown herself in the millpond after her husband took up with another woman; *Connecticut Gazette*, September 14, 1814.

4. Charles O. Paullin and Frederic L. Paxson, *Guide to the Materials in London Archives for the History of the United States Since 1783* (Washington, DC: Carnegie Institution, 1914), 37; W. Freeman Galpin, "American Grain Trade to the Spanish Peninsula," *American Historical Review* 28, no. 1 (October 1922): 33; Stewart to Barclay, June 23, 28, May 26, 1813, Box 6, Thomas Barclay Papers, MS 43, N-YHS.

5. Stewart to Barclay, May 19, 21, June 4, 9, 16, 23, 1813, Box 6, Thomas Barclay Papers, MS 43, N-YHS.

6. Barclay to Transport Board, May 20, 1813, George Lockhart Rives, ed., *Selections from the Correspondence of Thomas Barclay* (New York: Harper & Brothers, 1894), 331; Stewart to Barclay, July 3, 1813, Box 6, Thomas Barclay Papers, MS 43, N-YHS; Mason to Monroe, June 26, 1813, Dennison et al. to Monroe, June 29, 1813, Fairchild to Monroe, July 1, 1813, noted in Daniel Preston, *A Comprehensive Catalogue of the Correspondence and Papers of James Monroe*, vol. 1 (Westport: Greenwood Press, 2001).

7. Stewart to Barclay, October 8, 1813, Box 6, Thomas Barclay Papers, MS 43, N-YHS; they named the child John Carden Stewart, after their houseguest Captain Carden of the *Macedonian*, New London Vital Records; James Tertius de Kay, *The Battle of Stonington* (Annapolis: Naval Institute Press, 1990), 124-26 (Stewart also claimed to have been captured by a privateer, but the *Atalante* story sounds more plausible); *Connecticut Gazette*, March 23, 1814, a copy of Warren's February 17 letter was discovered in the boot of the captain of a Spanish vessel taken by the American privateer *Viper*.

8. *Connecticut Gazette*, November 16, 1814. Stewart is not specifically named in the brief newspaper report

of the sales vessel, but his presence, and the type of business, strongly support the supposition; de Kay, *Battle of Stonington*, 125-26.

9. De Kay, *Battle of Stonington*, 83; Dr. Samuel H.P. Lee of New London remarked on the presence of British officers and sailors in disguise in New London, and also commented there was little need for espionage as the British could easily see the situation from their ships, Samuel Griswold Goodrich, *Recollections of a Lifetime, or Men and Things I Have Seen*, 2 vols. (New York: Miller, Orton and Mulligan, 1857), 1: 484-86.

9. De Kay, *Battle of Stonington*, 83; *Connecticut Gazette*, December 21, 1814.

10. *Connecticut Gazette*, August 10, 31, 1814; her release was conditional on the end of British efforts to compel her release. Three weeks later the Stewarts' furniture was advertised at auction, either to pay family expenses or as a vindictive measure in their absence, *Connecticut Gazette*, September 14, 1814.

11. *Connecticut Gazette*, September 28, November 16, December 21, 1814. Mrs. Stewart claimed the amount was $200 and that Washington did not return the gold. The incident, depositions from the *Yankee* crew, and Mrs. Stewart's claim were covered in detail in the press because of the disagreement over whether Washington had returned the money or not. Washington may have deserted from HMS *Acasta* in 1813, and Mrs. Stewart knew he was living under an assumed name, *Connecticut Gazette*, September 22, 1813, December 21, 1814.

12. *Connecticut Gazette*, August 31, September 14, 1813; de Kay, *Battle of Stonington*, 193-94.

13. *Connecticut Gazette*, March 8, 1815; *House of Commons Papers*, vol. 37, *Accounts and Papers: Estimate; Army, Navy, Ordnance &c., Session, 15 November 1837-16 August 1838* (London, 1838), 117; de Kay, *Battle of Stonington*, 83.

SIDEBAR: **Hartford Convention**

1. Donald R. Hickey, "New England's Defense Problem and the Genesis of the Hartford Convention," *New England Quarterly* 50, no. 4 (1977): 587-604; Samuel E. Morison, *Harrison Gary Otis 1765-1848: The Urbane Federalist* (Boston: Houghton Mifflin, 1969), 354.

2. "What is expected of the Convention at Hartford. What it can do and what it ought to do," *Hartford Courant*, November 29, 1814; see additional articles under the same title on December 6 and December 13, 1814.

3. Jack Allen Clark, "Thomas Sidney Jesup: Military Observer at the Hartford Convention," *New England Quarterly* 29, no. 3 (September 1956): 393-99.

4. Glenn Tucker, *Poltroons and Patriots* (New York: Bobbs Merrill, 1954), 661.

5. Calvin Goodard to David Daggett, November 1, 1814, in William Buckley, "Letters of a Connecticut Federalist: 1814-1815," *New England Quarterly* 13, no. 2 (April 1930): 316-31. Theodore Dwight, editor of the *Connecticut Mirror*, a Federalist paper, stated that "secession was the last thing anyone thought of."

6. "Report and Resolutions of the Hartford Convention, 1815," in Theodore Dwight, *History of the Hartford Convention: With a Review of the Policy of the United State Government which led to the War of 1812* (n.p.: N.J. White, 1833), also available at http://www.lexrex.com/enlightened/laws/hartford_conv.htm, accessed March 2012.

7. See "Report and Resolutions of the Hartford Convention, 1815."

8. Donald R. Hickey, *The War of 1812: A Forgotten Conflict* (Urbana: University of Illinois Press, 1989), 256-57.

SIDEBAR: **Glorious Tenth**

1. Unlike Stonington's battle flag, the iconic "Star Spangled Banner," displayed at the Smithsonian Institution, does not have any holes from enemy shot. That flag was raised on the morning following the bombardment to the strains of "Yankee Doodle." Donald R. Hickey, *Don't Give Up the Ship! Myths of the War of 1812* (Urbana: University of Illinois Press, 2006), 88.

2. *Connecticut Gazette*, August 23, 1815, quoted in J. Hammond Trumbull, *The Defence of Stonington Against a British Squadron August 9th to 12th, 1814* (Hartford, 1864), 42.

3. *New London Gazette*, August 18, 1824, quoted in Trumbull, 42-43.

4. *Stonington Yankee*, reprinted in the *Norwich Courier*, August 24, 1825.

5. Courtlandt Palmer, oration at the 1883 observance, quoted in *Stonington Mirror*, August 11, 1883.

6. Ira Hart Palmer, cited in Henry R. Palmer Jr., "The Tenth of August Celebration," *Historical Footnotes* (quarterly publication of the Stonington Historical Society), August 1976, 13.

7. "Grand Celebration of the 62d Anniversary of the

BATTLE OF STONINGTON," program announcement, original at R.W. Woolworth Library, Stonington Historical Society; *Stonington Mirror*, August 17, 1876.

8. *Stonington Mirror*, August 11, 1883.

9. Henry R. Palmer, ed., *The Stonington Battle Centennial* (Stonington: Palmer Press, 1915); *Stonington Mirror*, August 13, 1914.

10. Program Brochure: 1934, original in Woolworth Library, Stonington Historical Society; Williams Haynes, ed., *The Stonington Chronology 1649-1949* (Stonington: Pequot Press, 1949), 121; Haynes, 133; Souvenir Program: 1964, incorporated in *Historical Footnotes*, August 1964, 1.

11. Palmer, "Tenth of August Celebration," 13.

Index